Exploring African Themes
in fabric and stitch

A thread follows the path of a needle.

Exploring African Themes
in fabric and stitch

Mary Sleigh

ISBN 978-1-904499-32-9

Further copies of this book may be obtained from
www.lizard-dance.com

Acknowledgements

I am very grateful to Lindsay Hooper of Iziko Museums in Cape Town and Julia Charlton of Wits Art Galleries, Johannesburg, for access to the museum collections and the time they spent sharing their knowledge with us.

Many thanks to Binky Newman and Stephen Long for their contributions to this book which are very welcome additions. My thanks also go to Jean Oliver, a fellow textile artist, for allowing me to include examples of her work.

This book could not have been written without the help, enthusiasm and encouragement of many people in southern Africa who have introduced and welcomed us into their communities. Our thanks go, in particular, to Koos Verwey, Graham Stevenson, Marc Baker and Emmanuel Njawa, who have acted as our guides and introduced us to the Himba of Namibia and the Maasai in Tanzania.

All the African artefacts, beadwork and textiles featured in this book are part of the personal collection of the author unless specified otherwise.

Photography by Roger Sleigh

Hausa robe detail on previous page

First published in Great Britain in 2009 by Roundtuit Publishing, 32 Cookes Wood, Broompark, Durham DH7 7RL.

Printed and bound in Great Britain by Falcon Press (Stockton-on-Tees) Limited.

Contents

Introduction

People often ask me how my interest in Africa started. Like lots of good things it started by chance! I was born in India and spent the early years of my childhood in the West Indies, so travel was part of my upbringing. On getting married I inherited a family who lived in the Cape in South Africa. However, I had never visited Africa and now there was an opportunity for me to see something of this vast continent.

My first impressions were coloured by my introduction, by my husband's family who loved the outdoor life, to the African bush and the vast unspoilt spaces of the Cape. We were lucky enough to be independent with a vehicle, an old Combi, and camping equipment at our disposal. Those early experiences struck a chord with me, and the people, places and culture have been a source of interest ever since. I learnt a lot about the flora and fauna, life in the bush and how to be self sufficient. In those days we were free to explore to our hearts' content and go where our interest took us, which was a great privilege. An adventurous spirit and opportunities to explore and learn about new and different environments, resulted in some exciting expeditions over many years. An environment and culture so different from my own made a great impact on me and continues to inspire my studies and creative work.

OPPOSITE: Karitu, a Himba woman.

As our family grew up we were able to go further afield and be more adventurous, so one thing lead to another. Once we left the cities and urban areas behind, it was easier to meet people who were willing to introduce us to some of the more traditional tribal people. As a visual artist, designer and maker, I was captivated by the ingenuity and skills of some of those more isolated groups. My interest has grown over more than thirty years and I continue to be inspired by their innovation and deep understanding of their surroundings.

Babati Mountains, Tanzania.

The visual impact of the landscape is there for everyone to see as soon as they step on African soil. However, in this

Introduction

book I am concentrating on practical craft skills as well as the appreciation of materials in the widest sense.

Making skills are an important part of everyday life in African communities. I have been impressed by the way their knowledge and experience are passed on from generation to generation. There is a noticeable decline in traditional skills, due to outside influences and changes in life style. There is an urgency therefore, to introduce, celebrate and promote the skills that still exist.

I feel very passionately that traditional practical skills should be valued as they are part of our heritage. It is not surprising that I was thrilled by the willingness of many of the women to demonstrate their talents as you can see in this picture of a Maasai woman showing me her beadwork techniques.

I had a carefree childhood with space and freedom to explore, with no technology or modern amenities and very few play mates within easy reach. Using my imagination to invent games and imaginary characters were a natural part of growing up. I came from a family who were good with their hands, had a sense of beauty and an appreciation of things that were well made, so practical skills were always encouraged. Being resourceful and using what was available were necessary and I now realise that it was a wonderful basis for nurturing creativity. Perhaps my upbringing encouraged me to embrace the culture of the small communities that we have visited in some of the more remote regions of southern Africa. My way of thinking and working has been influenced by exposure to their willingness to change, their resourceful approach, their understanding of their surroundings and what it has to offer. I hope I have brought to life something of their creativity, imagination and innovation. They are goals worth pursuing for artists, designers and makers.

A Maasai woman demonstrates her beading skills to me in Tanzania.

Chapter 1
Materials

Materials including raphia, barkcloth, woven grass fibres, leather and paste resist on cotton.

The focus of this chapter is an innovative and lively approach to fabrics, fibres and other materials to encourage investigation. My appreciation of materials in the widest sense has increased over years of research, study and time spent with groups of people living in more remote parts of southern Africa. In this chapter I have included examples of some of the many craft skills and materials that are important to everyday life in African communities. Practical skills are still passed on from generation to generation but that tradition is threatened by changes in lifestyle, increased travel and the influence of western culture.

Let's look at how a heightened awareness of the qualities of materials stimulates the creative juices, leads to experimentation and suggests new ways of working.

We'll start by considering some of the fabrics that provide such a visual feast as soon as you step on African soil. Textiles are as important as other visual arts and remain a dynamic part of everyday life as they constantly change and evolve, embracing new methods, materials and imagery. Fabrics that started as traditional cloths have become popular in the international market and are now exported across the world, contributing to the local economies.

Textiles have been an important part of the African import and export trade for centuries with a long history of trade between West Africa and the UK, Europe, Asia and Indonesia. Over the centuries there has been a cross fertilisation of cultural ideas, textile techniques and design and, increasingly, printed fabrics

Commercially produced printed fabrics.

Mowambu street market in Tanzania.

are now manufactured locally. Stalls with fabric for sale are a great attraction in local markets where people meet and can buy everything from a padlock to a goat!

In the crowd there is a buzz of excitement and the traders offer a feast of colour and pattern for those who want to buy, collect or just enjoy the atmosphere. Amongst the array of fabrics, there are imported as well as locally produced lengths of material. Many are printed and others are dyed and treated with a variety of resist techniques to produce decorative designs.

A fabric stall in Mowambu street market.

Indigo-dyed cloth is one example that has universal appeal, and is not only highly prized in Africa, but also around the world. West Africa is an important centre for growing cotton and indigo, so raw materials are readily available for weaving and dyeing. Indigo, grown widely, has the advantage of being

a substantive cold water dye needing no mordant. Historically, Nigeria has long been the centre of indigo dyeing and even though natural indigo has been replaced by synthetic dye, traditional methods are still in use there, as well as in Mali and Burkina Faso.

OPPOSITE:
Indigo-dyed fabric.

Indigo dyeing is an interesting process and started me thinking about ways to develop my own way of working. For those who live in colder climates woad is ecologically friendly and is a good alternative to synthetic indigo, although the pigment from woad is less concentrated than that obtained from tropical indigo. The woad plant, *Isatis tinctoria,* is a biennial plant originating from the Mediterranean and has been grown in Northern Europe and the British Isles since the Iron Age and probably longer than that. There has been a revival in growing woad and a renewed interest by designer-makers in using it, as they become more aware of environmental issues affecting their working practices. It is very simple to grow in a reasonably sunny situation, self-seeds very readily and grows so abundantly that it can become a problem weed!

The folk lore about woad and the alchemy of the dyeing process intrigue me and encouraged me to explore the possibilities of using woad as a natural dye to produce the subtle range of blues that are so appealing. I experimented using dried woad balls but had limited success and suspect I needed to do much more experimentation. There are many enthusiastic dyers who have experience with natural dyes who

A selection of fabrics dyed with woad.

might have more success! I have found out by trial and error and suggestions from dyers and suppliers that I can achieve a lovely range of blues using woad powder. This is the recipe I used to dye threads and fabrics in a bucket.

Recipe

> 5 litres water
> 60g washing soda
> 10g Hydrotherm DD (Hydros)
> 15g woad powder

Method

» Pour 5 litres warm water (about 30° C) into a plastic bucket.

» Add 60g washing soda and stir until dissolved.

» Gently sprinkle 10g Hydrotherm DD (Hydros) into the water and stir until dissolved.

» Slowly sprinkle 15g woad powder into the solution and stir gently until it is fully dispersed. This takes time.

» Cover the bucket with cling film and leave it for at least 1 hour.

» When the dye vat is greenish blue it is ready to use.

» Submerge fabric or threads in the solution and leave for 5 – 20 minutes depending on the strength of colour required.

Tips

» Prepare all the fabrics and threads before you start!

» You will achieve better results dyeing small quantities with the suggested recipe.

» Wear gloves and protect all surfaces to avoid staining.

» Weigh all chemicals and woad powder with care. You may choose to wear a mask.

» Don't use any kitchen equipment that you might need in food preparation.

» Use an old wooden spoon or stick for stirring.

» Ensure all fabrics have been washed to remove any dressing or use fabric that is sold as 'ready to dye'.

» Soak fabrics well in clean water before dyeing to allow the colour to penetrate the fibres.

» Add fabrics to the dye bath gently and ensure they are fully submerged.

» Washing soda is available from supermarkets.

» Woad powder and chemicals are available by mail order from suppliers, some of which are listed at the end of the book.

As the fabric is removed from the dye bath there is a magical moment when oxidisation occurs and the colour changes from yellow to green and then to blue. The more often the fibres are submerged in the dye bath the deeper the blue becomes.

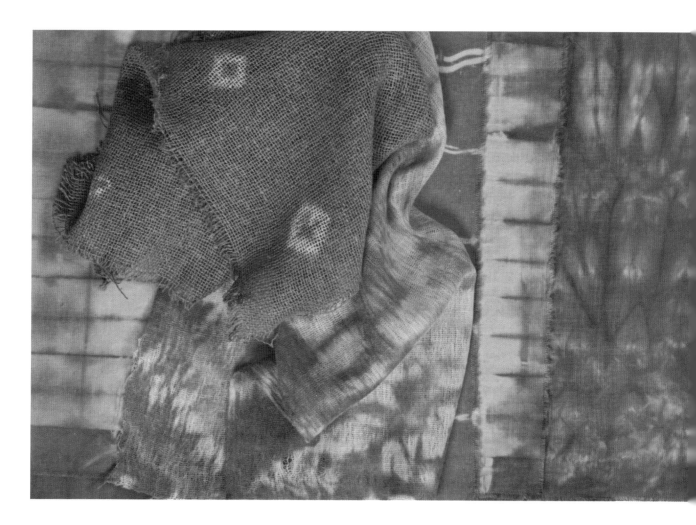

Woad-dyed fabrics using resist techniques.

Part of the fascination and frustration in the woad dyeing process is the uncertainty of the result but it's worth persevering. I experimented with calico, fine cotton, muslin and various types of silk, resulting in a range of soft and subtle blues. Silk scrim and muslin produced soft, delicate blues quite different from the dramatic dark indigo cloths that inspired my experiments.

Once you have prepared the dye bath it can be used on many occasions before it is exhausted, so you can have endless hours of fun. I prepared a variety of fabrics and with some I used stitch resist techniques similar to dyed cloths from many parts of West Africa. You could try hand and machine stitching to create fine patterns or tie-dyeing techniques which give bolder results.

OPPOSITE: contemporary
adire eleko.

Adire cloths are also dyed with indigo by the Yoruba women
of south western Nigeria, who produce them using a resist or
tie-dye method. When fine cotton material became available
through trade with Europe the Yoruba men developed a resist
technique using cassava paste. This was known as *adire eleko*
where designs were painted or stencilled on to the cloth with
the starch paste to prevent the penetration of the indigo dye.
The patterns were revealed after dyeing, when the cloth was
dry and the starch scraped and washed off the surface. The
most beautiful examples of *adire eleko* were superseded by
other multi-coloured cloths in the 1960s and are now difficult
to find.

The starch paste resist technique, however, is well worth trying
and is a simple and inexpensive way of producing a patterned
surface. In *African Inspirations in Embroidery* I have described
the textile technique in detail for those who are interested
in working on fabric. However, it is also very effective when
used on paper and relies on basic practical skills and involves
very little expense. Specialised equipment is not necessary as
normal household utensils produce very effective results.

Examples of papers using
the flour paste technique.

You will need:

- » A smooth working surface
- » Selection of brushes
- » Jam jars or similar
  containers
- » Scrapers, spatulas or
  marking tools
- » Inks, dyes or other soluble
  colour pigments to mix
  with the paste

- » Sheets of paper,
  preferably smooth and
  non-absorbent
- » Saucepan, wooden
  spoon
- » Starch or flour
- » Liquid glycerine
- » Liquid soap

Preparing the paste

Use one measure of starch to nine of water or one part of flour to five of water to prepare a jar of paste. To avoid lumps, start by mixing a small amount of water with the flour or starch, before adding the remainder of the water. Once you have a smooth mixture, bring it to simmering point, stirring all the time until it reaches boiling point and then allow it to thicken. Let it simmer for a few minutes rather like a white sauce! Take it off the heat and add a dessertspoon of glycerine and liquid soap, mix well and allow to cool. It is not an exact science but the addition of liquid soap and glycerine gives a smooth paste and helps to fix the pigments. Now you are ready to add colour to the paste. Proportions of paste to pigment depend on the intensity of colour you require. Liquid colour can be added directly to the paste, while tubes of paint or powder colour need to be diluted with water first and then added and mixed well. It's worth trying out some samples on scrap paper first, before working on your final pieces to see if the effect is what you want.

Now you are ready to start applying the coloured paste to the paper. There's no need to be too hasty as the paste mixture is slow to dry and you can work over the surface as long as it is wet.

Method

» Lay the paper flat on a smooth work surface.

» Load a brush with coloured paste and cover the paper evenly right up to and over the edge.

» Repeat this with other colours in separate areas, or at random, if you want a multi-coloured background.

» Draw, press or scrape into the wet surface to produce patterns.

» Use any tool that will leave a mark when dragged through the surface.

If you don't like the result, brush it out and start again.

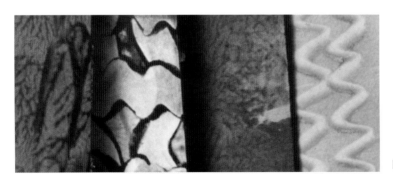

Detail of paste resist papers.

Too much paste may weaken the paper and too little will dry too quickly! Experience will tell you how much to apply.

Lay the decorated papers on newspaper to dry completely. They tend to curl up so when dry they should be placed under weights to ensure they remain flat.

The papers are now ready to use and work well as end sheets or covers for books. They are ideal for boxes, greeting cards or add an individual look to the presentation of projects. Diagrams and instructions for the boxes can be found at the back of the book.

Boxes made with decorated papers and one on the left made with burnished indigo fabric.

Tips

»   Collect all your equipment and prepare your work area before you start.
»   Use a clean brush to removes any lumps from the paper surface before working into the paste.
»   Use separate brushes for each colour, otherwise you will end up with murky results!
»   Remove any surplus paste from your tools before using them again.
»   Plan ahead as the papers need three or four hours or even longer to dry.
»   Never use dyeing equipment for cooking or vice versa.
»   Paste can be stored for several days in a screw top jar in the fridge.

Textiles are part of everyday life in Africa and a length of fabric has enormous potential as the Maasai demonstrate with the *shuka;* a simple length of fabric wrapped and tied around the body. A married woman wears three, while girls only wear two.

Maasai preparing for a *shirahe* or party.

Kangas are another example of how versatile lengths of fabric are worn by women, used as baby slings, or even to communicate powerful messages. The swathed and draped fabric looks stunning when worn for special occasions, or as everyday wear commonly seen in the towns and villages of East Africa. They are most often worn by women, rich and poor alike, although men wear them too, in the house rather than outside. Because they are easy and comfortable to wear, no matter what your size, not surprisingly, they are popular with tourists.

Colourful printed kangas are bought in pairs; women wear one tied under the arms around the body and the other around the shoulders and sometimes over the head. The kanga is a rectangular piece of printed cotton with a border and a central motif often incorporating some words. These slogans, mottos or messages are very significant to the design and very eye catching too. It is intriguing to try to work out the meaning of a slogan on a kanga when worn by a women walking down a street or shopping in a market! Kangas are often used as a powerful tool in creating public awareness about health education or promoting political issues.

The edge of a kanga showing the border and printed slogan.

Incorporating ideas and text, as an element of design, into our own work, gives us an opportunity to engage on another level with our audience.

Recently, I have become interested in the inclusion of text in my own work and have some suggestions for you to try out for yourself. Simple, direct printing on fabric or adding words or text with transfer paints and crayons are familiar techniques, but technology has opened up other possibilities. I have experimented with using my computer and printer to print directly on to fabric with some success after a lot of trial and error. Using a normal Word document either in landscape or portrait format I chose a suitable font and size of print for the words I wanted to include into a textile piece. It's very easy to experiment with options and try them out on paper before printing directly on to fabric. Once I had decided on the version that I was going to use I stiffened the fabric and fed it through the ink jet printer as if it were a sheet of paper and was delighted with the result. My printer does not seem to have suffered as a consequence but be cautious if you try this process!

Fabric sheets are now widely available that have been treated so that you can print directly onto them as if they were normal paper. They have a paper backing that helps to feed them through the printer and unlike my initial experiments the fabric has been pre-treated to fix the ink from the ink jet printer. They are supplied in A4 sheets of cotton, silk, linen and voile and are washable too.

I used cotton inkjet fabric sheets to print a series of our own photographs presented as luggage labels. Each one shows Maasai people accompanied by one of their popular proverbs.

OPPOSITE: *Maasai Labels.*

Computer skills open up the possibility of combining words or text with your own images or design work to communicate your ideas directly on fabric. Another method worth trying is transferring images or words by using heat transfer paper. Once your design work is resolved on the computer then you are ready to print the image directly onto the transfer paper. Remember that the image is inverted when transferred, so you need to select the mirror setting on your printer. By placing the image face down onto the fabric it is transferred by pressing down firmly with a hot iron on the back of the transfer paper. All these products come with full instructions and it is important to read them carefully before you start.

Sketchbook pages using heat transfer paper on fabric for the text.

A thread follows the path of a needle.

Happiness is as good as food.

You know what you will say but not what you will be told.

A man's deeds are greater than his birth.

Life cannot be hurried.

Materials

Another group of materials is made from fibres obtained from indigenous plants. These fibres are used to produce a range of materials that can be treated like fabric but have different qualities. Some, like raphia are woven in a traditional way to produce basic lengths of fabric that are transformed into patterned and textured pieces that are inspirational. Information about them is included in the next chapter.

Across Africa there are grasses, reeds and palms that provide the fibres for baskets and containers. I am amazed by the skills of those who work with these strong, springy, stiff fibres to create flexible materials, ideal for containers and three-dimensional items. Weaving, plaiting, coiling and wrapping are techniques common to textiles and basket making. The finished product is functional as well as decorative and has a 'feel' that is very appealing. All these qualities are evident in Zulu spoon pouches. They are woven with great care and attention to detail. They are used to hold spoons, ordinary utensils, that also have a symbolic importance for their owners.

Traditionally, adults had their own personal spoon carved out of wood. They used it to eat their basic food of soured milk or curds, while children would use their hands. The pouches are woven out of grass and embellished with beaded decoration on the surface and edges.

There is great satisfaction in designing and making something that is beautiful as well as functional. Here is a way of creating a basic material with some strength, rigidity and a crisp finish that closely resembles grass or reed fibres. I first learnt the basic technique from Linda Tudor, a fellow textile artist.

Traditional Zulu spoon.

Zulu spoon pouches.

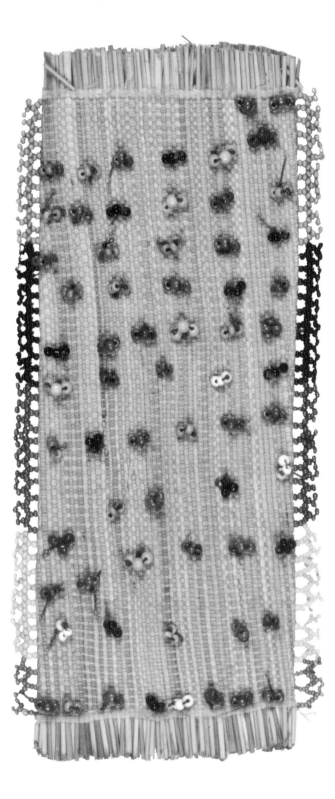
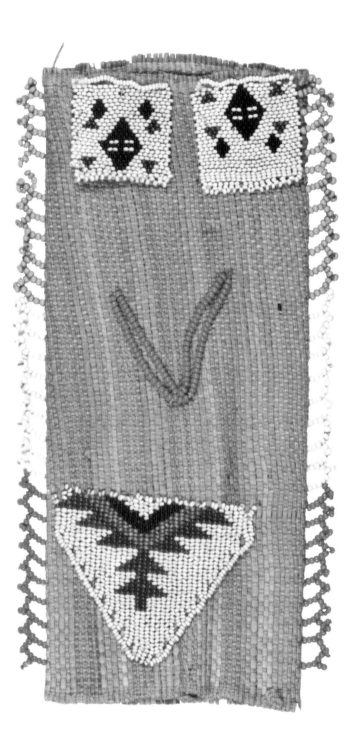

There are raw or tussah silks that have a strong linear quality and ridged texture that work well when stiffened. I treated some tussah silk with a PVA solution that gave a crisp, stiff finish when dry and used it for the pouch shown here and also for the samples inspired by raphia cloths that you will see in Chapter 2.

Method

» Make a solution of PVA and water to the consistency of thin cream.

» Brush it into the silk fabric so that it penetrates the fibres completely, right through to the reverse.

» Leave flat on a work surface or plastic sheet or hang it out to dry completely.

» It may darken slightly in colour.

» Once dry it will be crisp to the touch, transformed from a soft into a stiff fabric.

A pouch using stiffened silk and decorated with porcupine quills and ostrich eggshell beads.

Another category of materials widely used in rural areas includes animal skins and leather, particularly in arid regions where cotton or other fibres are not available. The preparation and treatment of animal skins involve particular skills and the knowledge and experience are passed on most often from generation to generation in communities that retain a traditional way of life.

OPPOSITE: Maasai man's leather cape decorated with beadwork.

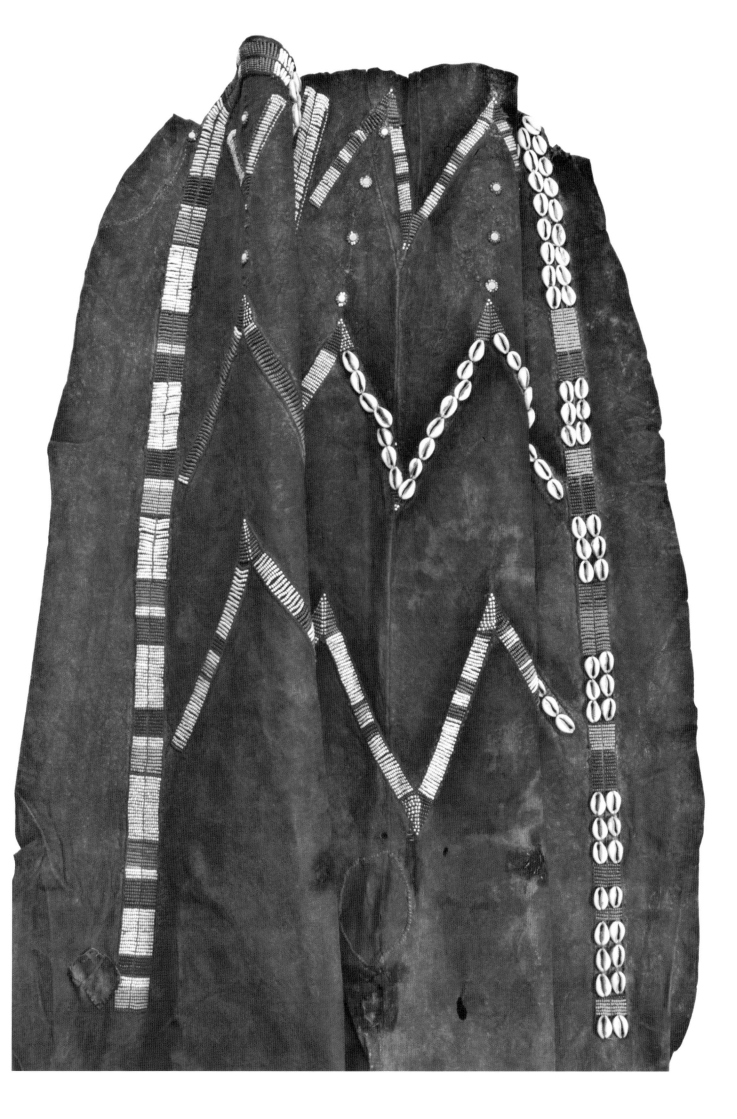

Materials

Charitable donations of second hand clothing however, are having an impact on customs and fashion, so jeans and T-shirts have become popular and more traditional costume is now only worn for ceremonial occasions.

Datoga headman with his wife and child.

The Datoga who live in Tanzania continue to use skins and are skilled not only in the preparation of the skins but also in the cutting, piecing and fitting of a garment.

You can see the complexity of the pattern cutting needed to produce the wedding cape opposite worn so proudly by the wife of the Datoga chief. The women in the village were also eager to show us how they began to prepare a goatskin by pegging it out and scraping it, before working on it further.

Detail of the wedding cape.

Beadwork is a favourite means of decoration used by the Datoga and Maasai on leather, adding colour and pattern to the natural palette. The Himba of north western Namibia also use goatskins and leather for clothing and body ornaments and these are immediately recognisable by their distinctive styles and designs. Their leather baby carriers and accessories are smeared with fat and ochre to keep them soft and supple, which is very similar to the mixture that they use to anoint their bodies.

Himba mother with a baby sling decorated with cowrie shells and glass beads.

Fabric and leather are similar in the way they can be sewn, folded, pleated, pieced, rolled and fringed. Leather is a material I enjoy handling because it is so versatile and so forgiving! Pushing the boundaries by experimenting with unfamiliar materials can lead to some unexpected results. The resourceful approach, so evident in the rural African communities that we have visited, of exploiting what is available, encourages me to look beyond my traditional materials for unusual or unexpected combinations of texture and surface. You will find some suggestions in Chapter 3.

Chapter 2
Construction

A collection of strip-woven cloths from West Africa.

For centuries West African countries have been highly regarded for their excellent weaving skills and in particular, for their strip-woven cloths. Many authoritative and well-researched books have been written about the methods of weaving and the technical details of the narrow looms. For those who have a special interest in the art of weaving in Africa they provide a wealth of information.

Traditionally men and boys are the weavers and women play no part in the process for cultural reasons. In *African*

Construction

Majesty Nicholas Barnard explains that "for the 'traditional' weaving cultures of West Africa weaving is seen as a god-given process, a manifest wonder of creativity, and the loom a divine instrument." There are many taboos surrounding looms and those who use them, one being that women could never be weavers as they have menstrual periods.

I have chosen the making of strip-woven cloths as an inspirational starting point and I find it is helpful to have a little background information to set the scene. The weavers use narrow strip looms that are small and portable, easy to set up and simple to use, so allowing the weaver flexibility and mobility. Ease of dismantling and removing the finished cloth for storage is important to their way of life. After weaving the long strips they are joined along the selvedge to produce a large piece of cloth and then a range of textile techniques are used to decorate them and create a patterned surface.

Many are dyed with a variety of resist methods, using starch, wax or stitch to produce a pattern, others are tie-dyed, painted or printed, all resulting in decorative surfaces. Mud cloths from Mali and indigo stitch-resist cloths from Cameroon and Burkina Faso are wonderful examples of the dynamic patterns that can be achieved by resist techniques.

Let's look at the strip-woven cloths made by the Ashanti and Ewe people of Ghana with their dazzling colours and woven details as starting points for developing ideas. They are a visual feast and even more spectacular when they are draped around the body and over the shoulder in everyday wear,

Detail of an indigo-dyed strip cloth from Burkina Faso showing the stitched seams joining the strips.

This indigo stitch-resist cloth from Cameroon and a mud cloth from Mali show the surface pattern achieved by resist techniques.

The Ashanti use dazzling colours in this kente cloth, contrasting with the more subtle Ewe cloth.

Construction

or worn as traditional dress for ceremonial occasions. They come alive as people move; the pattern and colours change and fragment rather like images in a kaleidoscope. These cloths have become familiar in the international market and are easily recognisable by the way woven strips of pattern are joined and blocks are aligned, to create a dynamic surface.

The Ashanti use dazzling colour combinations in the kente cloth on page 25, which contrasts with the more subtle palette of the Ewe cloth. The vibrancy and sophisticated colour combinations and patterns have an immediate impact and have long been a topic of interest and discussion.

When I first looked at the cloths in my collection it was those vibrant rhythms, intriguing composition and repetition of colour and pattern that appealed to me. On closer examination the apparently regular repetition turned out to be far from simple! However, it is the construction of these narrow strip-woven cloths that is the focus for this chapter, so let's look more closely at how these cloths are made.

These strips have been joined by hand but now more often are machine stitched.

The narrow width of the strips is very appealing but very labour intensive! The strips are commonly 10 centimetres wide although there are examples that are as little as 5 centimetres in width. As a construction technique it offers great possibilities as a starting point for experimentation. Making a large textile by joining strips, by hand or machine, is a technique that allows for unexpected alignments of pattern and colour, so serendipity plays its part! Traditionally the cloths depend on joining woven strips that are of similar width but you are not bound by the limitations of narrow strip weaving. With the boundless supply of available fabrics you could experiment with strips of varying widths. Instead of a woven design, you could use applied fabrics, embroidery stitches and embellishments to create pattern and horizontal stripes that reflect the designs that work so well in the Ashanti cloths, commonly referred to as kente cloths.

Detail of an Ewe cloth, showing the slightly raised stripes woven with thicker weft threads.

The Ewe people weave similar strip cloths, sometimes using a double weft thread in their designs to introduce a variation in texture to the horizontal surface stripes.

Construction

A similar effect could be achieved by creating a raised band with cords, braids or couched threads. In the example shown I have used silk fabrics to echo the lustrous surface and vibrant colours of two strip-woven cloths in my own collection.

Sketch book studies of a kente cloth with stitched samples using silk to interpret my ideas.

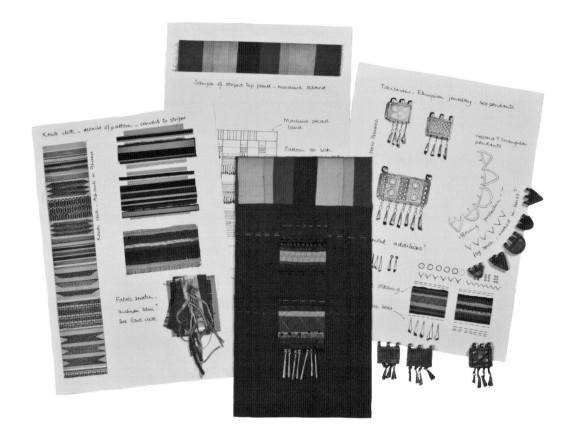

I developed some ideas from studies of Ashanti and Ewe cloths for this project. For additional interest I included some embellishments inspired by details from amulets worn by the Oromo women of Welo Province. To create the cross bands of colour and pattern I layered strips of silk, some had folded edges and others were frayed to introduce a hint of another colour. I added herringbone, fly stitches and beads to these coloured bands and then applied them to the vertical strips. At this stage I machine stitched the prepared strips to construct a larger textile piece.

Another West African strip-woven cloth worth studying for its construction is the adinkra cloth. I was originally drawn to it because of its blocks of printed symbols, most of which have a special significance. It is unusual because block printing is a less common method of creating pattern than the others I have already mentioned in this chapter. The stamps are made from pieces of calabash, a type of gourd, and a wooden comb is used to create the grid that divides the surface into

Tips

» Plan the composition of strips and intersecting bands of pattern before you start the project to estimate quantities of fabric. It's amazing how much fabric you need!

» Remember to use the straight grain of the fabric, particularly if you want to include frayed edges.

» Remember to add an allowance to all the seams for each strip.

Adinkra cloth from Ghana
printed and joined with
decorative seams

sections. Traditionally, adinkra cloths from Ghana are sombre
in colour to wear at funerals, whilst lighter, brighter ones are
used for happier occasions. The example shown here is a
pieced cloth using cotton strips of 40 centimetres, much wider
than those used by the Ashanti and Ewe people.

Construction

When I studied the adinkra cloth with some students and we looked more closely at its construction we realised that it was particularly interesting because of the way the strips had been joined. The seams are conventional in being turned in twice, but interestingly, are turned on to the right side and the turned edges are sewn together using a type of insertion stitch. It looks like the Half Cretan stitch illustrated in stitch dictionaries.

Detail of a seam showing the Half Cretan insertion stitch.

Instead of the seams being as unobtrusive as possible they are a dominant feature of the finished cloth. In this example, stranded cotton threads have been used in bright colours contrasting with the dull ochre background and dark printed symbols.

Detail of a seam showing the effect of the insertion stitch worked in brightly coloured stranded cotton.

A selection of embroidery threads that would give interesting effects.

Maybe you, like me, have had for many years a stock of stranded embroidery cottons waiting for the right project; here is an opportunity to use some of them! Most of us are spoilt for choice so the possibilities are endless. You can try using different types of thread as I have done in the samples and of course, use the insertion stitch itself as the source of more experimentation.

Another detail worth exploring is the way the seam allowance is folded on to the right side of the fabric adding interest to the finished fabric and becoming a significant part of the construction.

I padded the hems with some pelmet Vilene before stitching the seam together. Left to right, the sample shows some experiments using soft cotton, stranded cotton with mother-of-pearl buttons, perlé cotton with white glass beads, ribbon with old Xhosa metal beads and shiny knitting tape.

Construction

Try some of these ideas:

- » Use differing weights of thread.
- » Contrast shiny with matt threads.
- » Alter the spacing of the stitches.
- » Include a bead or button.
- » Pad the seam to make it more dominant.
- » Try bold contrasting colours.
- » Try closely matching fabric and threads.

Changing the threads:
Left to right: fine linen, perlé, space-dyed stranded cotton, soft cotton, thick twisted Perlita.

Altering the stitch:
Left to right: Grouping threads before completing the stitch, threading the needle with two different coloured threads, doubling the locking stitch in the seam, including a bead in the stitch.

A pieced and patched ceremonial raphia skirt from the Congo Region.

Raphia cloth from the Congo Region has inspired artists and intrigued textile enthusiasts for more than a century. The length and width of the woven cloth are restricted by the length of the fibre stripped from the palm leaf. Longer and wider pieces can be constructed by piecing and patching sections of the woven fibres.

In the piecing process the hems are intentionally turned onto the right side, so raised edges and hems are important in the construction of the finished textile. They become a decorative feature adding texture to create a lovely tactile surface. The sections are joined using a knotted stitch.

It is similar to a coral stitch and to achieve the result found on the old raphia cloth skirts it is important when stitching to insert the needle at right angles to the seam or hem. You will

Construction

discover that this stitch is very versatile as it works well for hems, joining sections and appliqué and makes a decorative edge too. You can see how it has been used as a way of applying shapes in the image of the ceremonial raphia skirt on the previous page and in the detail of a panel I worked on dyed cotton, which I then treated with gesso.

Detail of the knotted stitch used on the hems and seams.

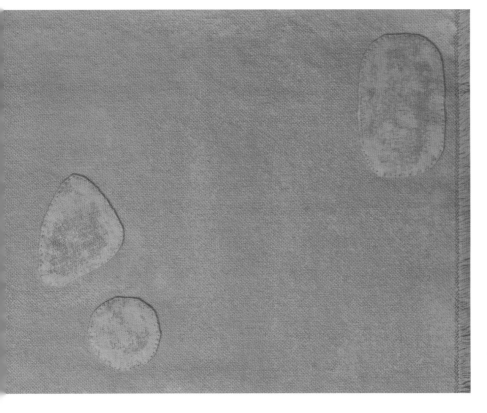

Detail from *Starch and Ochre*; I applied these patches with the traditional knotted stitch and then treated the surface with gesso.

The crisp, fibrous feel of tussah silk is similar to raphia cloth, so is an interesting fabric to use in a series of samples exploring ideas based on the techniques used in the ceremonial cloths from the Congo Region. Colour and tone are important parts of their designs so I used the natural toning colours of tussah silk to reflect those of the traditional raphia cloth.

The square patches are made of tussah silk and stitched together using perlé thread. The sample shows the effect of the knotted stitch in the seams and some of the hems.

In the samples, I stiffened the silk as described in the previous chapter, making it much easier to work with the small patches. Try using this way of joining patches and you will find they lie flat and the marks made by the stitches introduce another detail to the surface.

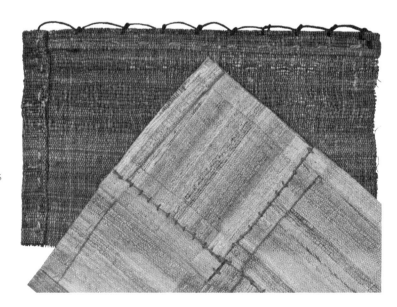

Alternating the direction of the grain of the fabric creates subtle changes in the square patches while the darker sample shows the knotted stitch worked more loosely as an edging.

Here is how to join two patches using the knotted stitch:

» Prepare the folded hems and secure with a running or knotted stitch.

» Place the wrong sides of the patches together. Remember, the hems will be on the right side!

» Work from right to left.

Step 1.   Step 2.   Step 3.

» Using a firm thread insert the needle through both patches near the edges to be joined and at right angles to them. (Step 1)

» Take the thread over and around the needle. (Step 2)

» Pull the needle through and pull the thread up firmly directly above the join. This locks the stitch and locates the half knot in the seam. (Step 3)

» Continue stitching by deciding on the length of the next stitch and then insert your needle a little further along and at right angles to the edges.

» Continue as before.

The completed join will lie flat when opened out with the stitch lying in the seam.

On the back there will be a line of small straight stitches across the seam.

I have always loved the feel of raphia cloth and am fascinated by some 19th century Shoowa currency cloths from the Congo Region, formerly Zaire, recently added to my collection.

Currency cloths from the Congo Region woven from very fine raphia.

I was intrigued to find out more about them and discovered that historians have a lot of evidence of purchases being regularly made using cloth as a currency. Cloth money had the advantages of being portable, easily divided and wearable, but could also create a storage problem and deteriorate with time, so cloth currency died out in the 1900s and was replaced by coins.

Construction

One of my currency cloths is a narrow piece made up of two strips of raphia cloth. It not only has a fascinating history but also inspires creative ideas by its construction. It's made of two finely woven strips of raphia with a darker chevron surface design on the right side so the turned seam joining the strips reveals the plain weave on the wrong side.

Surface pattern on the right side of the currency cloth.

Rather like the adinkra cloth, here's another example of the seam construction contributing a strong element to the design. The knotted stitch found in many pieced and patched cloths from the Congo Region joins the two plain bands running between the patterned sections which you can see in the narrow currency cloth. It is very unusual for raphia cloths to have a selvedge so the raw edge is turned twice and hemmed down. Amongst our own hoard of fabrics there are some that have an interesting selvedge that could be exploited as a decorative feature.

I have used the knotted stitch in the seam with the selvedge showing on the right side.

» Could you use the selvedge as a feature in a constructed piece? Printed fabrics are sometimes plain on the wrong side so that could provide a contrast when the seam is turned onto the right side.

» Slubbed fabrics have wonderful irregular selvedges that catch the eye, and when the undulating edges are visible they demand special treatment!

I have used the selvedge of slubbed silk as a feature of the hand stitched seam with recycled brass rings as decoration.

Construction

Traditional Xhosa cotton skirt
made in the mid 20th century.

Hems and seams are an important element in the design of the traditional skirts and tobacco bags made by the Xhosa and Thembu of the Eastern Cape in South Africa. The costumes and accessories made by them are very distinctive with strong contrasts of black on white.

The skirts and tobacco bags are made of thick white cotton with contrasting black stripes, some are applied, others are made of beads with beaded fringes and rows of tassels, all adding weight to the garment. Applied black strips cover the skirt seams and narrow stripes are repeated around the skirt to create decorative bands of pattern.

The stripes are often punctuated with mother-of-pearl buttons so beloved by the Xhosa speaking people.

Mother-of-pearl buttons introduce an interesting detail to the design on a Xhosa skirt.

Both men and women used tobacco bags and the examples shown overleaf were made in the 1950s and 60s by the Thembu. They were originally functional items to carry a home-grown supply of tobacco and a pipe and a few small items. They became fashionable accessories that were much sought after and a man might wear several on a girdle or around his neck to signify status and wealth.

Construction

Xhosa tobacco bag with pocket flaps, bead decoration and applied strips.

The selvedge detail has been incorporated into the two pocket flaps on the bag below.

Distinctive black cotton binding conceals the seams and defines the shape of the bag. The same black cotton is used for the fine hand stitched stripes, which are repeated in beadwork techniques that are such a strong element of Xhosa surface design. Most bags have one or more side pockets with the decorated pocket flaps integral to the whole design.

The Xhosa used the same cotton, sometimes called cotton baise, to make their nursing charms worn by nursing mothers to ward off evil and illness. The cotton fabric was ideal to make into soft rolls sometimes fringed at one end. Cotton cords were threaded through the rolls of fabric and brought together to form a decorative panel complete with tassels. By threading beads between the cords a soft flexible fabric was constructed; the whole piece being suitable for a nursing mother.

A collection from the Eastern Cape of Xhosa nursing charms made in the 1950s and 60s.

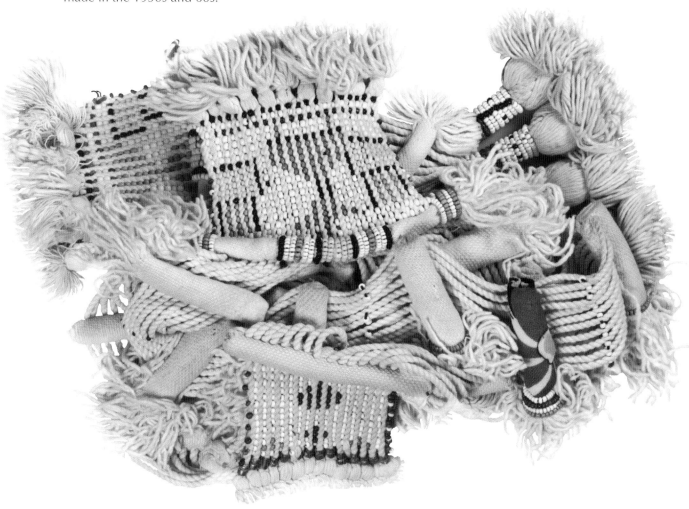

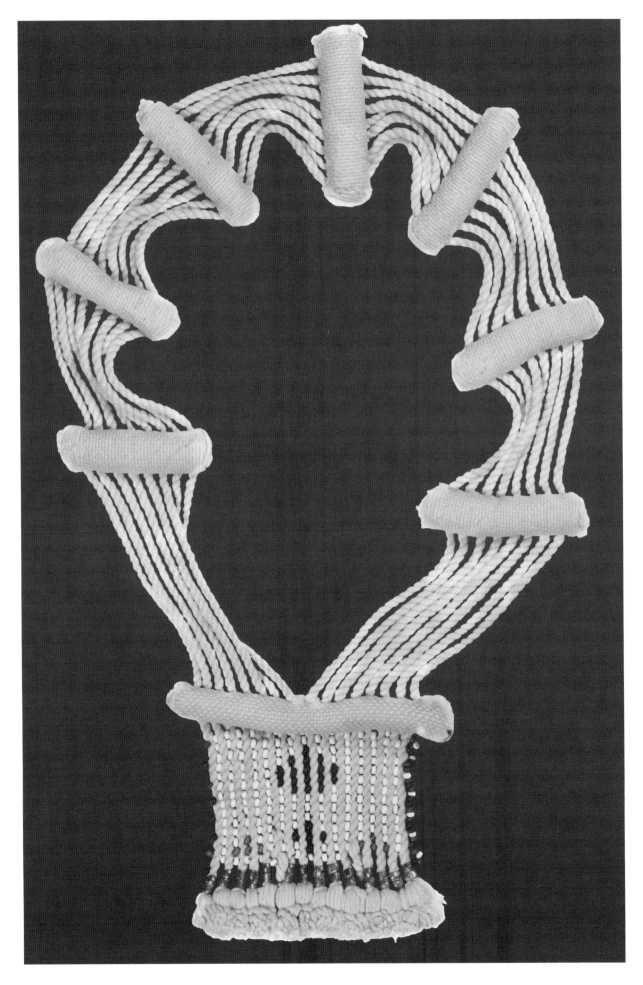

The construction of the decorative panel or amulet itself is worth studying and suggests all sorts of ways of embellishing a fabric to make a decorative feature.

Detail showing the construction of the cords and rolled section.

Soft beaded decoration using a typical geometric motif.

OPPOSITE:
Xhosa nursing charm from the Eastern Cape.

You could experiment in a similar way using cords, braids or rouleaux with beads in between. The idea of making a soft, flexible beaded fabric appealed to me and I tried an experiment using a loosely woven silk tussah instead of cords as a structure to hold the beads. I chose Czech beads which naturally vary in size to complement the uneven texture of the slubbed silk, on the next page. Once you start experimenting you will discover endless variations on this theme that exploit fabrics which provide an open structure or grid. This allows the beads to sink into the weave rather than sit on the surface.

Construction

Once you start experimenting, ideas begin to flow and you will think of many more using your own skills, experience, and materials.

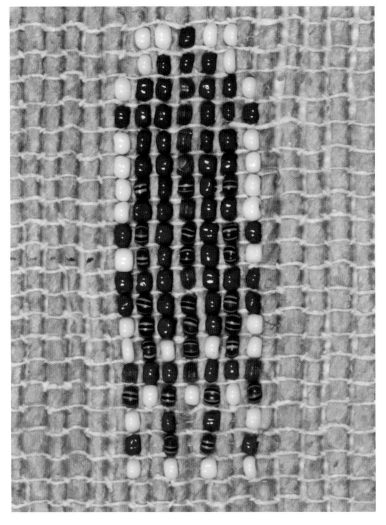

I used loosely woven tussah silk as a base fabric with glass Czech beads in this experimental sample.

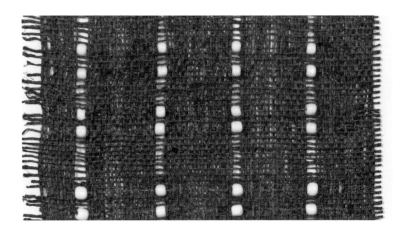

Warp threads have been withdrawn from the hemp ground fabric and used to weave white Czech beads into the surface.

Warp and weft threads have been withdrawn from this fine coloured canvas and used to stitch blocks of coloured beads into the fabric surface.

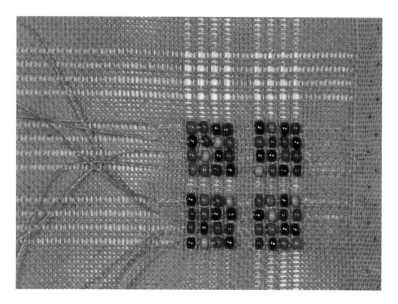

Try some of these ideas:

» Withdraw threads from a woven fabric and insert beads in their place.

» Withdraw either or both the warp and weft threads to achieve different effects.

» Include the beads using the withdrawn thread that matches the ground fabric exactly or alternatively choose a contrasting thread.

» Waxing the thread not only strengthens it but also makes it easier to weave through the spaces.

» Work on a larger scale using a large gauge canvas or even rug canvas.

» Paint or spray the canvas first to give a coloured background.

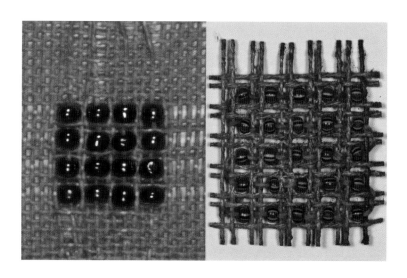

I explored some different ideas by using blocks of a single coloured bead on the fine orange canvas and changed the scale by using rug canvas which I sprayed with metallic paint before inserting the beads.

Binky Newman

Visitors to *Design Afrika* are presented with an Aladdin's cave of finely crafted items. Tucked away in a quiet cul-de-sac in Woodstock, Cape Town, is a gallery shop filled with beautiful baskets, sculptures, textiles, stools, jewellery and hand made artefacts of all sorts. *Design Afrika* was established in 1995 by Binky Newman whose vision, was to present examples of the finest traditional crafts to the widest audience.

Binky first fell in love with baskets when she travelled through southern Africa as a student and continues to be passionate about ensuring that basket making skills survive. Baskets from southern Africa and as far away as Ghana and Burkina Faso fill the shelves in her shop. Some are simple and austere, made of dried, faded grass; others are big and bold, richly coloured, decorated with cowrie shells or coloured beads. 'African baskets have got soul and that makes them unique' she says, 'but baskets survive the ravages of time least well – they are so organic that they melt away into the earth.' She has been working with rural and urban groups for more than twenty years to assist them with business training and to encourage product development. Younger women realise that there is the possibility of generating income for their family and that helps to ensure that traditional skills are passed on. Experience, knowledge and customs are preserved and adapted to appeal to the changing market place.

Binky has recently designed a contemporary range of baskets. The inspiration came from a traditional basket made by the Xhosa people in the Eastern Cape which is used to carry vegetables. The indentation in the bottom helps the basket to rest on the head, whilst the twisted grass cord can be used to carry the basket when empty.

This moulding of the shape of the basket gave Binky the idea to construct a much larger basket based around a wire frame. Professor Pedro from Zimbabwe constructed the wire frame which was sent by bus to the Eastern Cape. During the journey the frame was bent into an irregular shape. On arrival in Coffee Bay, the Masizame weavers thought the misshapen form was meant to be like that, so Notuzile Makaula, a 70 year old traditional Xhosa weaver, wove around the bumps and dents without straightening the wire form. Another journey by bus back to Cape Town produced yet more bumps and dents, and this is the result.

Binky decided to leave the irregular shape of the basket alone and has chosen it as an inspirational piece for its wonderful organic form, irregular shape and texture.

A traditional Xhosa basket (45cm high).

Detail showing the indentation and carrying cord.

A contemporary basket designed by Binky Newman (70cm wide x 80cm high).

Chapter 3
Recycling

Recycling has long been part of a way of life for African people, not because of the problems of waste disposal but through lack of resources, necessity and limited incomes. They are open to possibilities and a resourceful approach is widespread, and perhaps because materials are limited, innovation plays its part. I hope you will be encouraged to take a similar approach after you read this chapter. I can still remember very clearly the wonderful picture of a family shelter in Namibia constructed out of soft drink cans. It had

Shelter made from soft drink cans,1992.

been made by a Damara family who were trying to earn a living by acting as guides to travellers who had come to see the ancient rock carvings at Twyfelfontein. On a more recent visit in 2007 it was nowhere to be seen, as this area has been developed as a World Heritage Site and there is now a visitors' centre where the shelter once stood.

Rock carvings at Twyfelfontein.

I know from my own experience that I work most creatively when I have to make the most of what I have and am not diverted by too many choices! The 'I wonder what would happen if' question often leads to a freedom of approach and unexpected results in our own creative work. A search through the contents of our own desk drawers, tool boxes and garden sheds could open up possibilities for our own work.

Everyday needs in African villages lead to recycling. Visitors to rural areas cannot go far before realising that walking is a part of everyday life for most people in the more remote regions of southern Africa. For those who are more fortunate, bicycles are a popular form of transport and trucks are becoming more common. However, the Himba in Namibia and Maasai in Kenya and Tanzania still walk vast distances daily, so it is common to see them wearing sandals made from recycled old car tyres. They are a welcome and effective protection for their feet from stones and thorns along the tracks in the bush. The Himba often hang their sandals on the outside of their hut for safety, as you can see in this picture taken in Kaokoland in Namibia.

Himba sandals.

Recycling

Family meals are an important part of the rhythm of life and cooking pots are used regularly on the fire. Battered and worn out old aluminium saucepans used to be the main source of metal for the Maasai women to make small decorations to include in their beadwork.

Nairoshi, a Maasai woman, wearing her beadwork.

Something that struck me, when we were sitting round a fire at night in a Maasai village, was the way beads glistened and the metal shapes reflected the flickering firelight, adding a magical touch to the dancing, which is such an important part of any celebration. I love the beadwork where each metal shape has been cut by hand out of discarded aluminium cooking pots. Each piece is unique and more appealing than the commercially produced discs that are stamped out in a factory and are now widely available in local markets.

Detail of Nairoshi's earrings.

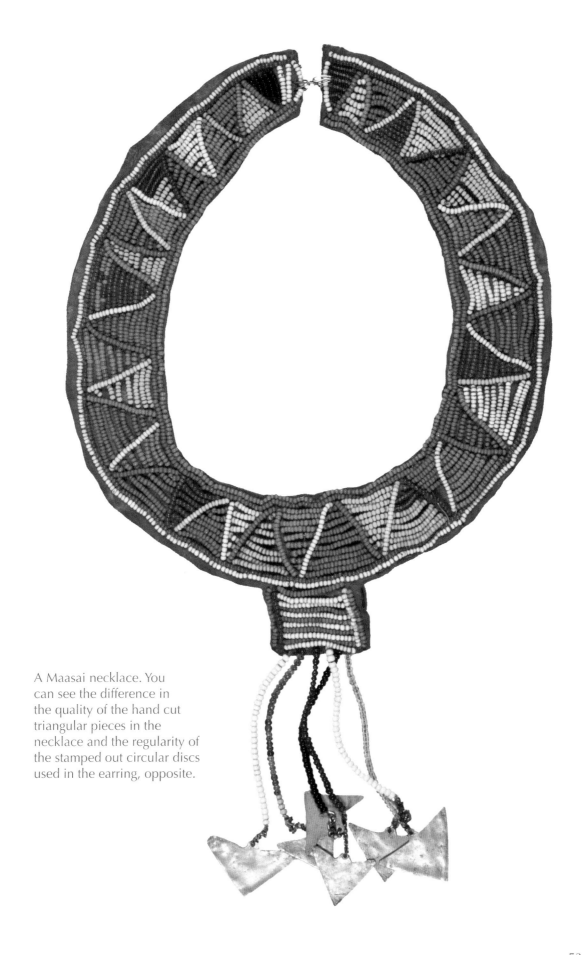

A Maasai necklace. You can see the difference in the quality of the hand cut triangular pieces in the necklace and the regularity of the stamped out circular discs used in the earring, opposite.

Recycling

Recycling is part of life for the Datoga who live in Tanzania and are mainly pastoralists. However, quite unusually, a small group, work as blacksmiths. They have a separate area for their work situated at a distance from their huts. They use bellows made of animal skins, set up to direct the air through a clay funnel to a small charcoal fire. The men take it in turns to work the bellows to create sufficient heat to melt old padlocks and other recycled objects. When molten, the metal is poured into small troughs, cooled and then beaten into shape. They make arrow heads, *pangas* or machetes and jewellery for local people, including the Maasai.

Datoga jewellery.

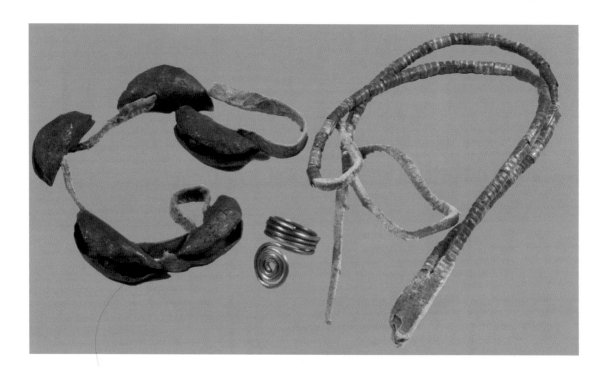

Detail of anklets showing the construction of the 'bells'.

Another man often accompanies them, making music by plucking a bow using a gourd as a sounding board. Metal beads and anklets are very popular and are also made from recycled plastic.

When we met the wife of the village headman and blacksmith, she was delighted to show us her jewellery, a status symbol of her position in the community.

Datoga woman and her jewellery.

Recycling

Metal does not deteriorate when discarded in arid regions and so it is not an unusual sight to see junk lying in these isolated areas. What is rubbish to one person has possibilities for others and is waiting for someone with initiative to use! Recycling and an imaginative use of found objects are integral to the design and making of Himba body ornaments. During an expedition to a more remote part of Kaokoland, I was intrigued to see how a Himba woman had incorporated an old zip into her goatskin skirt, just for its decorative qualities, rather than as a method of construction. While walking in the bush it is possible to find spent metal cartridges left lying after shooting expeditions. They are just the perfect size and shape to be included in a decorative hairpiece and even old drawing pins are not too humble to make a point too! The hair piece shown here is worn by a girl after puberty, whether she is married or not. It is called an *oruvanda* and made to traditional regional patterns. Once it is completed it is smeared with *otizumba*, a mixture of charcoal, cooked fat and aromatic plants.

The ability to see possibilities in the most unexpected objects is a great asset to the creative process and something to encourage in our own thinking. Even the metal beads used in this hairpiece are interesting. Each one is hand made by an itinerant bead maker. We were lucky enough to be visiting some small village communities in Kaokoland when he arrived. He came with wire and a few simple tools which he used to cut and form the metal beads, each one beaten out by hand. They are traditionally used for all the body ornaments that the Himba wear, so he had plenty of custom and was paid in kind according to the number of beads sold.

Oruvanda or hair decoration.

Itinerant bead maker in Namibia.

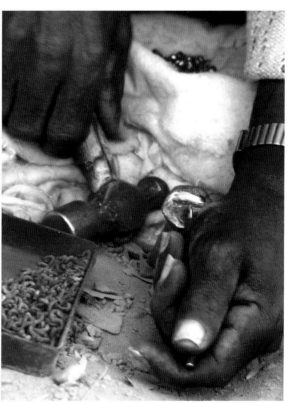

Detail of the bead maker at work.

Recycling

It's surprising what you can find when you search through your store of things kept in the hope that they will come in useful one day! I had stored a roll of copper, probably originally for use in electrical work, which had been retrieved when clearing out a garage. The picture of the bead maker came to mind as it occurred to me that the copper would lend itself to manipulation.

Work in progress.

I decided to investigate the possibilities of incorporating the copper into my textiles by treating it in various ways to express my ideas. There was something attractive about the smooth, flexible metal surface that could provide an interesting contrast to the soft feel of fabric. The smooth surface can be textured by beating, embossing and scratching. The malleable metal lends itself to folding, rolling and can be cut, pierced and punched.

I found that small copper sections worked well as a contrast to hand made paper or fabric. Most recently, I included some copper additions to a group of bags called *Conversation Pieces*.

This collection is a celebration of friendships made over many years with groups of people living in remote parts of southern Africa. It expresses something of the common language that binds us, with each copper motif being repeated, with variations, on each of the bags.

OPPOSITE:
Conversation Pieces.

58

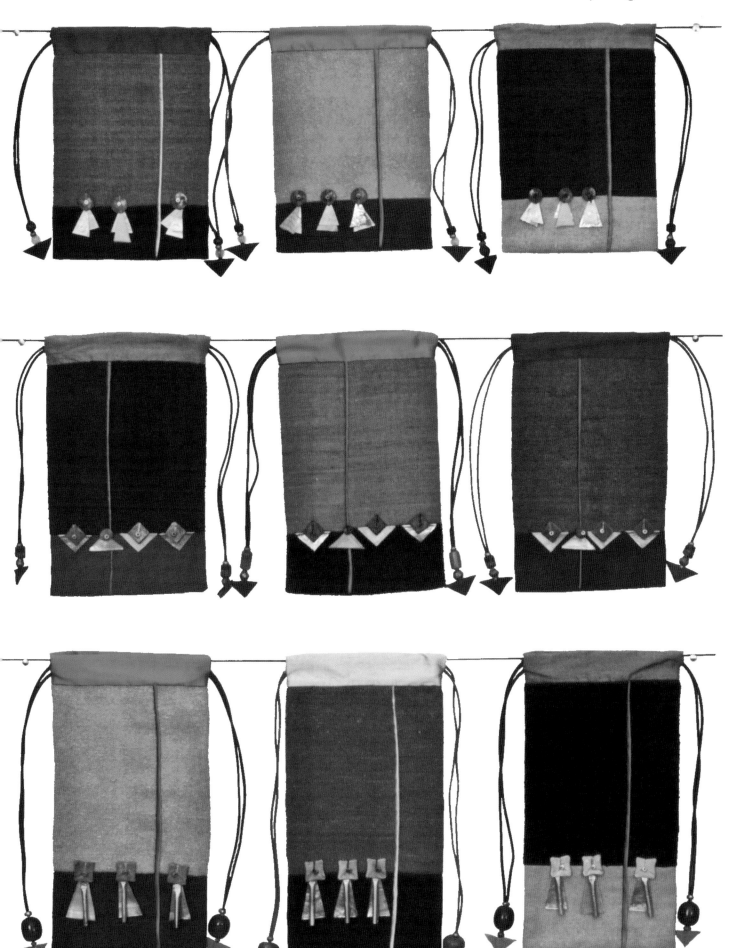

Recycling

I have a collection of old brass washers that came from a traditional piece of Xhosa beadwork that was broken and past repair. It was a Xhosa Thembu pubic apron, known as *izinkciyo,* which would have been worn by a Thembu woman under her skirt. These beaded aprons were made during the 1940s up to the late 1960s with Venetian glass beads and brass washers, which were sold to them by European traders.

Xhosa Thembu beaded apron.

I wanted to use and recycle the washers but they looked too perfect and uniform. I had discovered some interesting effects achieved by using patina aging solutions, when experimenting with the bare copper metal, so I tried it on the washers. I applied some fluid to the bare metal, which is formulated to create a blue patina, and soon achieved the colouration you can see in the first sample, quite different from the untreated ones in the second sample.

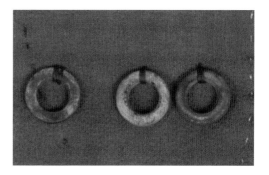

Two samples using recycled brass washers.

Recycling

Discarded aluminium drinks cans and tomato puree tubes provide another source of metal for us to recycle and can be opened out and washed ready for use. Be careful of the sharp edges on aluminium cans when you cut them open. Tools such as pliers and wire cutters from the tool shed are more effective implements than our normal sewing equipment and much safer too!

A variety of thin sheets of metal and mesh are available from suppliers for those of you who would like to explore these ideas but have no metal to recycle. I have created some interesting results with copper, brass and aluminium, treating them in the same ways as my old roll of copper. The smooth, bright, shiny surface may not be the effect you want, so try some of these techniques.

» First clean the metal with a metal polish to remove finger prints and oils used in their production.

» Place the sheet of metal on a pad of newspapers and indent them on the back with a ball point pen or emboss, beat or scratch the surface with suitable tools.

» Punch holes, pierce with a needle or cut with scissors.

» Apply shoe polish or acrylic paint to add colour.

» Colour brass and copper by holding it in a gentle flame with wooden tongs. A gas flame on the cooker is suitable. Dip the metal into water to stop the colour spreading.

» Aluminium can be softened, but only turns black and may melt if held in a gas flame.

» The thinnest metals can be sewn with care by hand or machine.

Of course, iron rusts naturally and copper tarnishes but it takes time and the right conditions. You can speed up the oxidisation process by using patina aging solutions or a rust activator to create a weather-worn look.

Jean Oliver, a textile artist who enjoys using mixed media is currently including metal in her work. She was inspired to experiment with a range of metals when she attended workshops in USA tutored by Mary Hettmansperger. By heating and then treating copper and brass with the patina aging solutions, she has achieved a wide range of colours in *Look no Stitch*. The effects work very well with the bright elements of untreated copper contrasting with the subtle colour palette of the textured and treated metal.

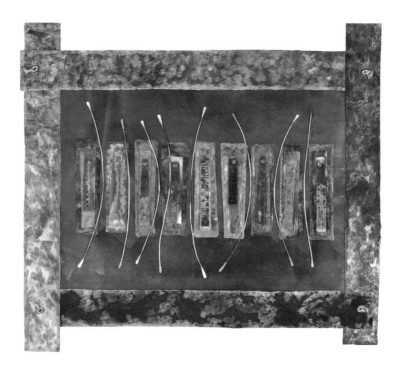

Look no Stitch by Jean Oliver

There is a range of metal effect water-based paints on the market, which contain real metal particles and can be used on non-metal surfaces, which will tarnish over time when exposed to the air. I used metal effect iron paint, bronze powders with acrylic paint and patina aging solution on paper clay, which completely altered the colour and surface. I have included more about paper clay in chapter 4. The antiquing or patina aging solutions are water-based acidic solutions which work very well on metal effect paints. They react with metal or real metal particles in metallic paint to produce an aged patina, in a variety of colours, depending on the type of solution.

Tips

»   Read the instructions and safety notes carefully before starting to use the solution.

»   Treat with care and avoid contact with skin and eyes.

»   Protect work surfaces and wear gloves.

»   Apply directly with a brush or sponge on to a bare metal or metallic paint surface while it is wet.

»   Allow to dry naturally and leave to oxidise.

»   A thin coat of lacquer or varnish will help to retain the coloured surface.

Recycling

Large numbers of migrant workers still continue to leave their homes in the rural areas of the Eastern Cape to find work in the cities, mines and factories. In the past, when they returned home they often brought back small items and gave them to the women in their families to incorporate into beadwork, clothing or accessories. Here you can see how two small discarded glass bottles have been used to make a Xhosa beaded container for love potions. A larger Zulu container, originally containing pills, has been decorated in a similar way.

Two beaded containers using recycled items.

Many of these indigenous artistic traditions have been adapted to appeal to the tourist market, so instead of beadwork being used for personal adornment, it is now used to decorate functional items such as bottles and mugs. Historically men used wire to decorate walking sticks and staffs which were traditional accessories. More recently, migrant workers use wire and plastic-covered telephone wire to make items for sale in local markets. The baskets woven in this way have become highly collectable and are now sought after for their colour, pattern and form.

Recycling buttons has been widespread for a century or more and the Zulus, among others, exploited the decorative possibilities of metal buttons. They were probably gathered from discarded military uniforms as you can see in these Zulu anklets made about 70 years ago. They introduce a contrasting colour, surface and scale to the beadwork and of course, make a sound when the anklets are worn for dancing during a celebration.

A discarded button, metal washer, key or electrical component can take on another identity when included in a textile or piece of beadwork. They may have an interesting shape or texture and can introduce a personal touch to your own creative work. The Iziko Museums in Cape Town have a large collection of Xhosa beadwork. While studying the collection I was delighted to find some wonderful examples of unusual recycled items.

Zulu anklets.

Recycling

An old spoon and a whistle have taken on a new life as decorative items in these beadwork necklaces. The collection below shows the more familiar combination of beads with mother-of-pearl buttons, but what an inspirational idea to use the plastic tops of toothpaste tubes!

A recycled spoon included in a Xhosa necklace.

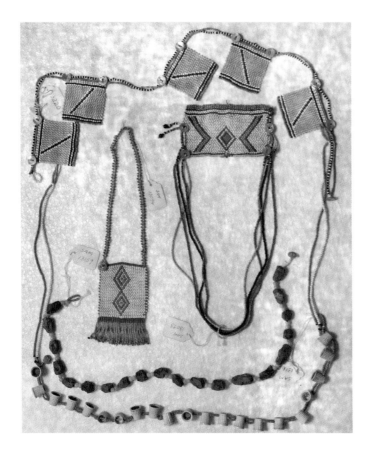

Xhosa beadwork and necklace incorporating a whistle.
Beadwork on this page from the collections of Iziko Museums of Cape Town, South Africa.

Buttons have been applied with great effect on clothing, accessories and included in beadwork by the Xhosa for generations. They would probably have been recycled from discarded clothing worn by the original settlers. They have a distinctive style of decoration with mother of pearl buttons being an integral part of their designs as I have mentioned in the previous chapter. Buttons, military or domestic, have shanks or holes for easy attachment so are ideal to apply! Quite recently I used an old box of buttons as inspiration for *Buttoned Up*, a concertina book. Ideas started to flow from the contents; not just about the buttons themselves but also the marks they leave on the cards, the holes and methods of attachment.

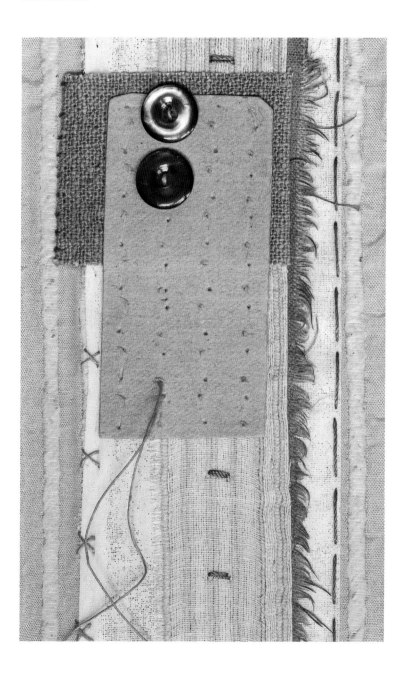

Detail of *Buttoned Up*.

Recycling

It's not just man-made items, but the natural world too, that offers an endless supply of things to recycle. I'm sure I am not alone in being a magpie! It's a universal habit to collect and take delight in searching for treasures along the beach or in the countryside. These found objects have a special significance for the person who finds and collects them. It is very often the colour, texture or shape that catches the eye and stimulates the imagination. Often it is not the right moment to draw or record ideas but useful to pick up a stone, shell, feather or leaf that says something about the place or occasion. The things I collect are personal and important to me but are not rare or precious – a note of caution there! To others they may seem useless or even rubbish, but to me they are tokens and memories of people and places I have visited, just waiting for the right moment to be used.

I have found that during visits to more remote villages in semi-arid desert areas the less you carry the better! On

A collection of some found objects.

these occasions my small sketchbook doubles up as a diary
to record immediate impressions and fleeting glimpses of
things that have disappeared long before I could draw them.
I have found these notes hastily scribbled down very useful,
together with the found objects I have collected along the way.
They help to conjure up the feelings and atmosphere of the
moment. Several weeks, months or even years go by before I
start to unravel the ideas, images and scraps of information.
Gradually ideas begin to take shape and the collection of
found objects become a valuable resource.

A whistling thorn bush.

Thorns cannot be ignored during hot and dusty walks in the
bush in Namibia, where thorn bushes and acacia trees are a
characteristic part of the landscape.

I have often collected thorns as they are easily found, though
not always welcome, in the desert. Because they are so
evocative of their environment and make such a telling mark I
have included them in several textile pieces.

Thorns used as a surface mark.

Recycling

While walking, porcupine quills can be found too, and appeal to me for their shape and markings and are particularly useful because they come in many sizes. The long straight ones worked well as hanging devices or as hinges when I used them in a series of hand made books. I discovered that they can be applied with couching stitches or pierced with a needle and thread. They are also easy to cut into varying lengths to make beads to apply as a surface decoration. Recently I have noticed that they are available to buy in shops, so others have recognised their decorative qualities too.

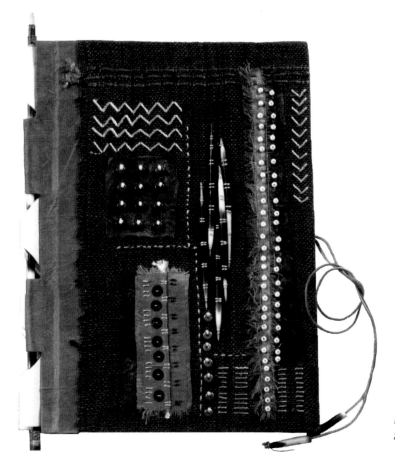

Porcupine Book with quills as hinges and decoration.

The Bushmen are believed to be the oldest inhabitants of southern Africa and now live a very different life, having been forced out of their ancestral homes in the Kalahari. They have learnt the new skills of growing vegetables and cattle farming as they can no longer sustain their traditional way of life as hunter gatherers. Historically, it was the men who were the hunters and the women the gatherers. They depended on hunting and plants for food so their nomadic existence was very logical, in that it followed the seasons and the availability of ripening foods and sources of water. Their way of life harmonized with nature and they had a wide knowledge and deep respect for their natural environment. It was a necessity of life that the men developed hunting, stalking and tracking skills while the women learnt to recognise where to find edible roots or tubers deep underground and of course the most important resource of all – water. Perhaps it was from this knowledge and that life was hard, that they made such good use of what was available to them in what used to be an isolated region.

African tortoise.

Tortoises are native to the bush and as well as a favourite source of food for the Bushmen, the shell makes an excellent container. The small tortoise shell shown here was made into a container for a powder of ground fragrant herbs or seeds complete with a small powder puff made of animal fur. It is decorated with beads rather like the Bushmen bags and jewellery, an example of their love of decoration.

A Bushman tortoise shell powder container and puff.

They make a variety of pendants, necklaces and bracelets using natural materials gathered from the bush, such as seeds, berries, nuts and found objects. The fruit or nut from a makalani palm tree is often used as a large bead. It is commonly known as vegetable ivory, large enough to be carved and used for pendants not only by the Bushmen but also the Damara and Himba in Namibia.

A carved makalani nut.

The decoration is made by carving away the dark brown surface to reveal a light colour underneath. They have become popular with tourists and the designs have been adapted to appeal to that market.

A basket of carved makalani nuts.

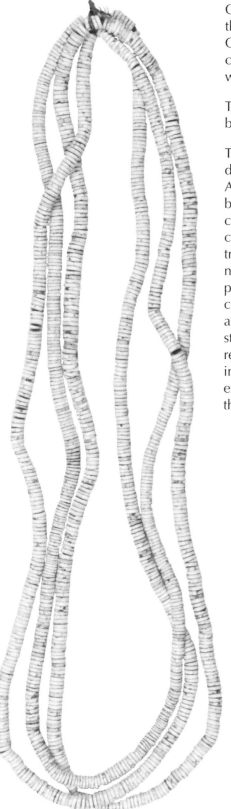

Ostrich eggs make delicious omelettes and Bushmen carry them home to provide a nutritious meal for their family. Once they are eaten, the shells are often used as ideal storage containers. They are plugged with a grass stopper, filled with water and stored under the ground.

The shell itself is a strong material that has been used to make beads for centuries using very simple technology.

The rough edges of the small fragments of shell are smoothed down to approximately the same size and shape with a stone. A drill, worked by a hand bow, is used to make a hole in each bead. Ostrich eggshell beads are becoming less common with commercially made beads now taking their place. The art and craft skills that were used by their own communities relied on traditional designs and materials, but rural communities are now buying factory made utensils, ready made ornaments and plastic beads. There is no longer the need for the old, time consuming activities, so there is a fear that these traditional arts will be lost. However, despite the changes in their life style, the old craft skills that can generate income are being retained through community projects and co-operative initiatives. Tortoise and ostrich eggshell buttons are an example of adapting natural resources to satisfy demands from the urban and tourist markets.

Ostrich eggshell beads.

Buttons made from tortoise shell and ostrich eggshell.

Chapter 4
Decoration

Xhosa beaded collar.

The love of decoration pervades all spheres of life among African communities and it seems as if nothing is too ordinary to be left unadorned. Our senses are bombarded by colour, surface pattern and texture which are not only visually but intellectually exciting too. Older textiles and pieces of beadwork speak of the past and are a record of styles and ways of life that have changed. There are many contradictory ideas that are put forward to explain the significance and meaning of the abundance of body ornaments. It is accepted, however, that styles of decoration do convey information about the makers and owners, their gender, social and marital status, and geographical origins. It is a changing world and hand made artefacts and many of the traditional craft skills are disappearing, as the role of girls and women change in their communities. Factory made clothing is relatively cheap and mass produced jewellery is readily available as plastic replaces glass beads and commercial interests motivate the market. However, public ceremonial occasions, festivals and rites of passage still play an important part in the culture of most communities. These are opportunities to retain their individual identities by wearing local costume and adornment.

A Maasai women would wear several of these neck collars as adornment.

What I find inspiring is that despite change, there are deeply felt sentiments and cultural values that continue to be invested by the makers in their crafts and remain important to the owners. Beadwork is still a vehicle for self expression that is kept alive by an innovative approach to design, a willingness to embrace changing styles and by incorporating new materials. Similar reasons for investing time and effort in the designing and making process could be starting points worth considering in our own work.

Decoration

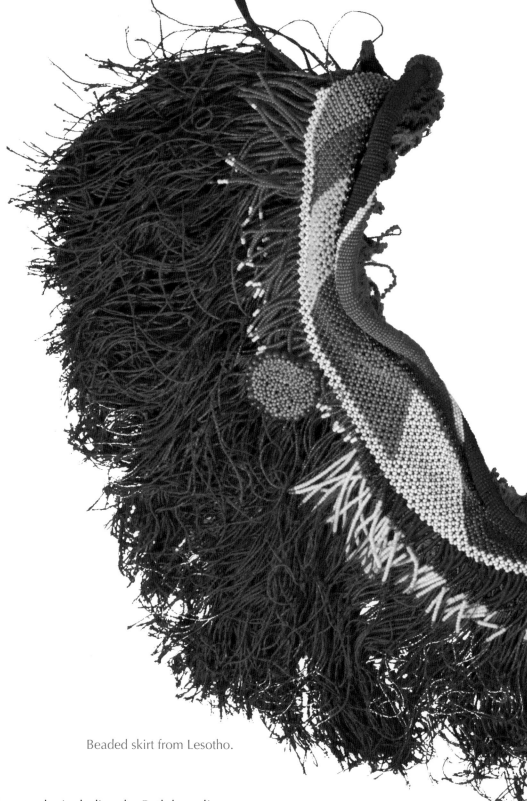

Beaded skirt from Lesotho.

The southern Sotho people, including the Batlokwa, live
mainly in Lesotho, a small independent country within the
borders of South Africa. The beaded skirt or apron shown here
would be worn by a southern Sotho woman from the Mount
Fletcher region close to the Drakensberg Mountains. It was
made in the 1960 – 1970s using Czech beads and plant fibres
rubbed with red ochre. Originally it would have been made
for her initiation ceremony, and then worn for her marriage
and after that for special occasions only. Having taken four or
five months to make, this is not an everyday item as you will
understand when you realise what is involved in the whole
process!

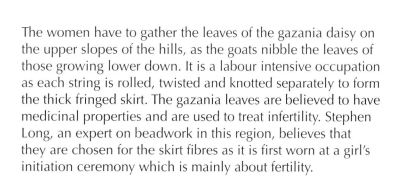

The women have to gather the leaves of the gazania daisy on the upper slopes of the hills, as the goats nibble the leaves of those growing lower down. It is a labour intensive occupation as each string is rolled, twisted and knotted separately to form the thick fringed skirt. The gazania leaves are believed to have medicinal properties and are used to treat infertility. Stephen Long, an expert on beadwork in this region, believes that they are chosen for the skirt fibres as it is first worn at a girl's initiation ceremony which is mainly about fertility.

The beaded belt at the top of the skirt is bought separately and made by specialist bead workers and as such is highly valued.

Decoration

Fringes, tassels and streamers are an important feature of decoration amongst many groups of people and adorn bags, beadwork, skirts and aprons.

Tassels are also a distinctive part of the design of Xhosa tobacco bags that are mentioned in Chapter 2 which range from small intricate beaded tassels, or individually twisted fibres, to long decorated streamers made of cords, beads or leather. The quality and materials depend on the article and the community, for whom these items hold a special significance. The long beaded or plaited cords and leather streamers signify that the tobacco bag would probably be used by a man, while women's bags have shorter tassels.

Tassels and
streamers.

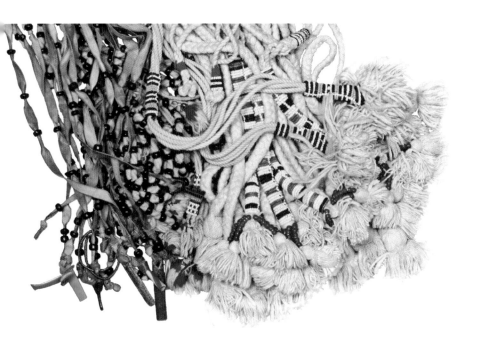

Xhosa beaded collar
cascade 40cm long.

Which ever technique is used, these decorations add not only colour, pattern and texture but also a dynamic quality of movement and sound when they are worn. The makers of these bags demonstrate their skills with imagination and innovation and there seems to be no end to the possibilities! Sometimes the bag is overloaded with decorated tassels, beadwork and found and recycled items.

Cotton cords are twisted in varying thicknesses, grouped and bound with beads, or plaited to include coloured wools. The ends are finished with a tassel which may also be beaded or knotted in various ways.

In contrast the old leather purses, made about the same time, in the 1960s, are much more austere. They were made in urban townships and bought by migrant workers as presents to take home to their wives. The long leather streamers are bound at intervals with hammered brass wire and finished at the ends with pointed brass caps. The face of the purse is decorated with brass studs and eyelets, which are included in the design at the top of the streamers and on the strap.

Fringes, tassels and decorative edges are also important features of Xhosa beadwork which is made by women and girls for their families and friends. The colour white was regarded, and is still valued by some, as a symbol of purity and associated with supernatural communications with their ancestors.

Some are head to toe adornments, such as the Themba chest cascade shown overleaf, and others are beautifully crafted double collars with intricate dangling strings of beads. Their designs include flat, flexible beaded collars varying in width, illustrated at the beginning of this chapter; quite different from the stiff wired beaded neck collars worn by the Maasai girls and women. Through exposure in the media those images have become very familiar, although they also wear a wide variety of other jewellery including arm ornaments with long beaded streamers especially for parties, as Kiendeti is wearing in the image overleaf. These move and sway as they dance and include chains and metal discs that add to the excitement and visual display.

Leather purse.

Decoration

Very often the only opportunity to see a wide range of
traditional beadwork is in museums where it is exhibited
flat. The pieces are accessible for study and beautiful to look
at but it is only when they are worn that they come to life.
Each individual piece conveys a lot of information about
the identity of the owner of the jewellery. Embedded in the
decoration are visual references to age, gender, marital status,
wealth and locality. Much of this information would not be
obvious to the casual observer, but the abundance of jewellery
worn by some individuals is a clear indication that the owner
is someone of wealth and status. It is not unusual to see
Maasai women heavily laden with several pairs of earrings,
neck ornaments, arm bands, bracelets and necklaces. Pattern
and colour overlay each other; a clear declaration of wealth
and prestige in their community. Included in the array there
are often symbolic pieces that indicate that they are married,
have children or have a son that is in training as traditional
warrior or *moran*.

Kiendeti wearing a
beaded arm ornament.

Xhosa Thembu chest
cascade 110cm long.

80

Detail of a moran's belt.

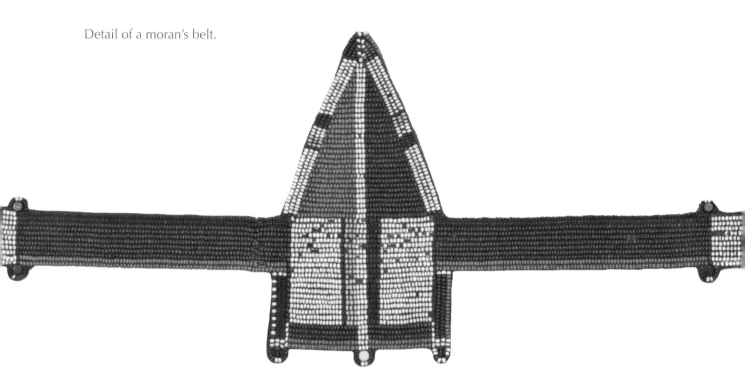

The men are also adorned with beaded items and celebrate the importance of their cattle with a decorative device on their belts, triangular in shape depicting a horn.

Inspiration for personal work comes from all these pieces with their innovative use of materials and extravagant displays of colour, texture and movement. I delved into my own supply of materials to explore ideas for making individual units that could be applied separately or grouped together to form tassels or decorative features.

I have already mentioned my interest in using metal and my own found objects. Here was an ideal opportunity to experiment with recycling some of the aluminium cans and, where appropriate, to include found objects from my collection. I discovered that the metal from the drink cans was very springy and difficult to manipulate but became more flexible once I had heated it in a gas flame.

Decoration

I rolled sections of aluminum to make long cylindrical beads and from a selection of cans chose parts of the printed surface that resulted in interesting patterns and colours. Others were made from rolled sections of sheets of copper, brass or aluminium shims. I treated the metal with some of the methods I have explained in the previous chapter and embellished the metal tubes with eyelets, wire, contrasting metal strips, threads and beads.

Their form and shape gave rise to the idea of using cinnamon sticks and porcupine quills as the core of the 'bead' and incorporating some of my found treasures. Matt acrylic varnish worked well in sealing the cinnamon sticks without making them shiny. I included my guinea fowl feathers picked up in the bush in Tanzania and peacock feathers gathered during our travels in India, to add colour and interest.

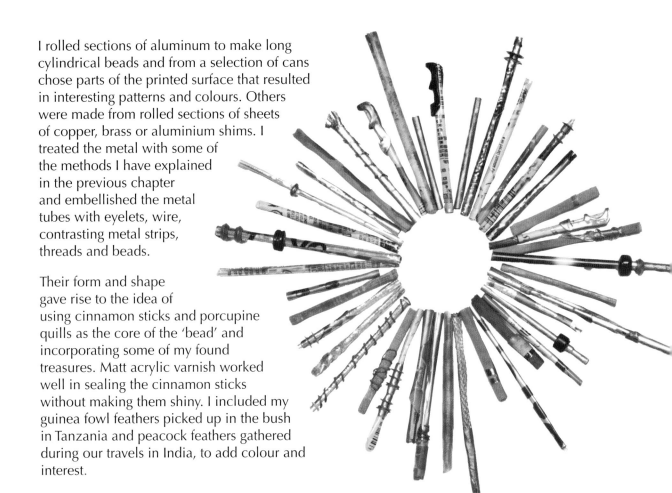

A selection of decorative items ready to be assembled.

Decorative items – found objects and mixed media.

On a more mundane level ordinary household items are commonly decorated with pattern and colour. Gourds are grown to use as eating and drinking bowls and are often painted with abstract patterns. They are also used as containers for snuff or medicine, the latter being used by a healer. The beaded snuff gourd in my collection was bought from a shaman in the Lady Frere District of the Eastern Cape. Shamans are believed to be intermediaries between humans and the spirit world and have healing powers.

A Xhosa beaded medicine gourd.

Milk gourds, ladles and containers of all sorts and sizes are necessities of life and have surfaces that are readily decorated. The Maasai decorate their milk gourds with beadwork and often repair them when they crack which implies that they are greatly valued.

A Maasai milk gourd showing a repair.

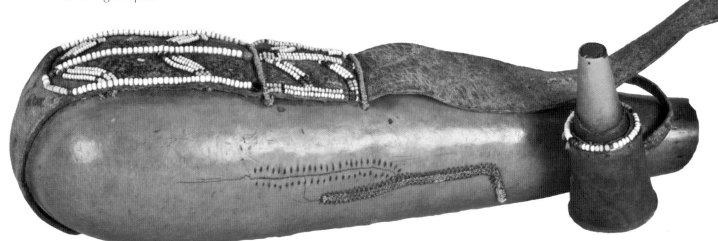

Decoration

Styles of pattern and design vary according to the traditions and natural resources of each region. Where wood is available it is used by local communities. Grass, reeds and palm fibres are ideal for making durable, lightweight and inexpensive baskets, mats and brushes. The art of basket making seems to be universal and is especially interesting to textile enthusiasts as there are many similarities in the techniques we both use. Natural or dyed fibres, rather like threads, produce variations in colour and pattern, many of which are enhanced to appeal to visiting tourists. Farming communities use wide shallow baskets for winnowing, deeper ones to carry vegetables from the fields and huge woven containers for storage, most of which include decorative patterns in their design. Basket making skills are still alive in many areas and have been revived by the new and expanding commercial opportunities. What were once purely functional items have become sought after by visitors who appreciate the decorative qualities, the sculptural forms and traditional skills.

Detail of a basket made for export from Ghana.

Himba basket hanging outside a hut.

We are not alone in having a deep desire to make something with a purpose and there is a satisfaction and pride in something that is not only well made but is also useful. Use and purpose is the motivation for most crafts in African rural villages but decoration is integral to their production. During my first visit to Kaokoland in the north west of Namibia, I was captivated by the baskets used by Himba families in their communal family meals. They bring together the use of local raw materials and highly developed practical skills with an eye for form and function. Woven out of the makalani palm fibres they produce strong baskets with leather tags for hanging them safely out of the dust and to avoid damage by animals.

Once the women have cooked the mealie meal with milk and sugar to make 'porridge' for the family it is put into one of these woven containers or baskets. The family pass the container round for everyone to help themselves with a wooden ladle, so meal times are very much a social occasion. Despite their everyday function very often these baskets have a beaded decoration, similar in design to their body ornaments and made out of leather, hand beaten metal beads and cowrie shells. Above all it is the shape and form of the baskets that are inspirational, particularly for those who are interested in developing three-dimensional work.

A group of Himba baskets showing the decorative tags.

Shembe beadwork bands used to decorate headdresses.

The importance of identity is deeply embedded in the African culture, and there are many devices to communicate this information in visual ways. The Nazareth Baptist Church was founded in 1910 by Isaiah Shembe and created a unique fusion of Zulu and Christian theology. The members of this church known as the Shembe, retain a tradition of wearing beadwork, unlike other converts to Christianity. The predominance of white beads and colourful geometric designs are distinctive features of their style of beadwork. Superficially it is similar to many other traditions but the patterns and colours are clearly recognisable to other members of the church from far afield and other Christian groups who have given up wearing beadwork.

Sometimes a deeper meaning is not immediately recognised by the casual onlooker. For example, the Xhosa nursing charms in Chapter 2 (page 43) though decorative and quite complex in their construction, are worn by nursing mothers as amulets for their protective properties. Likewise, to the uninformed, it is not obvious that the patterns woven into the kente cloths from Ghana (page 25) had symbolic values and were intended to express a precise meaning as well

Decoration

A Maasai woman wearing a coiled necklace.

as an exciting visual display. Without searching beneath the surface of many everyday items we miss much of their significance. The sight of Maasai mothers or young warriors is stunning in itself but amongst the array of colours, shapes and pattern there are symbols and meanings that they hold very dear. Maasai women who wear flat coiled brass earrings or necklaces signify that they are married and a mother, and have significance to both mother and son.

She would lend the necklace to her son as a token during his healing period after circumcision.

Young men become members of an age set when they are all circumcised in a ritual ceremony. They go on to form strong bonds throughout their time as warriors and later in life until they die. As a badge of their age set they wear identical beaded anklets which look very unassuming but have great significance for them.

Maasai anklets.

Many of us have memories, tokens or items that have special significance for us; things we would like to keep or celebrate. Past generations had keepsakes, lockets, diaries and autograph books, that now give us a little window into their lives and what was precious to them. I have mentioned that the small things I collect have no intrinsic value but are wonderful reminders of people and places and provide inspiration much later for developing ideas.

I love words and books so have found ways of making book structures as a way of keeping and recording these ideas, which may be single objects or 'material sketches' for future development. The little *Concertina Book* works well and contains information about combinations of surface and texture that appeal to me.

Concertina Book.

I made my own book cloth for the pages as well as the end covers. The following method results in paper-backed cloth that has body and strength, is easy to handle and of course can be stitched.

To make book cloth you will need:

Fabric – remember to allow enough for turnings

Japanese paper larger than the fabric – a thin *kozo* paper is best for lining fabric

Paste – starch or rice paste is available from book binders

Paste brush

Soft roller – a sponge roller works well

Hand spray for water

Ruler

Decoration

 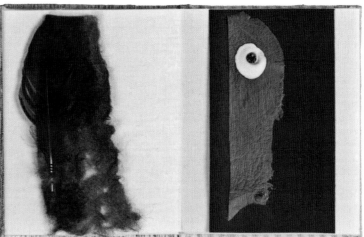

The cover and some pages of the *Concertina Book*.

Method

»   Prepare the paste to the consistency of mayonnaise.

»   Place fabric face down on a smooth clean, dry surface, laminated work surface or glass.

»   Spray the back of the fabric with water and smooth out any wrinkles.

»   Gently stretch and straighten the grain of the fabric.

»   Apply a thin layer of paste with the paste brush to the back of the <u>paper</u> spreading it evenly over the entire surface.

»   Place the ruler across the short end of the pasted paper, lift and turn it.

»   Holding the ruler, place the pasted side of the paper down over the fabric, covering it and the edges completely.

»   Use the roller on the surface of the paper to remove any air bubbles and try not to make any wrinkles!

»   This also helps the paper adhere to the fabric.

»   Ensure that the paper overlaps all the edges of the fabric.

»   All the outer edges of the paper should be pasted over the fabric to the working surface.

»   A small tab of paper placed under the long edge of backing paper helps to lift it when it's dry.

»   Allow to dry completely. It should dry taught with minimum shrinkage.

»   Insert a blunt instrument under the paper tab and lift the book cloth gently away from the surface.

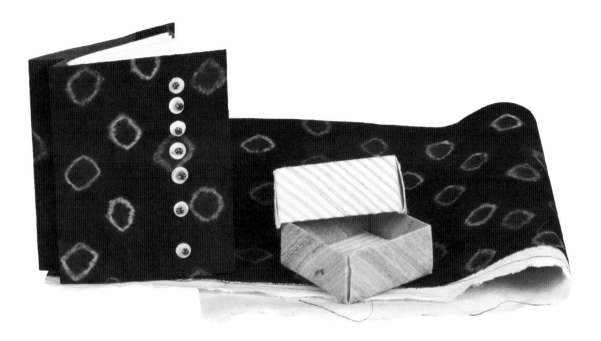

Soft book cover made with indigo book cloth and tussah silk used for the box.

You can use book cloth to make limp book covers or small containers similar to those suggested in Chapter 1, or to cover mount board for stiff end covers.

A book can take many forms as you can see in the small examples that Jean Oliver has made using metal for the covers. I find them very appealing as objects and reminiscent of amulets, preserving something precious to the owner and perhaps never revealed. It is that sense of mystery that intrigues me; that the contents may be open and informative but on the other hand could be secret, personal or have a special significance for an individual.

Jean Oliver's books with metal covers. Actual size.

Decoration

A sense of mystery is inherent in the study of fertility dolls, sometimes referred to as child figures or forms. I first saw a collection in the Museum in Cape Town and some time later at The University of the Witwatersrand Art Galleries in Johannesburg. I was able to study the Standard Bank African Art Collection which includes many 'dolls' or child figures.

N'wana (child figure)
Tsonga-Shangaan, South Africa
Wood, beads, fibre, textile, buttons.
Height: 12.6cm, diameter: 20.2cm.
University of Witwatersrand Collection.

The dedication at the front of *Evocations of the Child*, a book accompanying an exhibition of the same name, expresses most eloquently the wonder of these figures. It reads:

'Dedicated to the many unknown women whose aspirations, desires and sense of nurture were, and still are, lodged in these fragile figures that played a role in courtship, bonding of clans, evocation of children and, above all, focussed the human capacity to wish, hope and play.'

They were made by women for girls and not intended for public display. Of course girls would play with them, as children do all over the world, carrying them on their backs, tucked in at the waist or as a pendant around the neck.

Traditionally, they were made by women for use in the context of a woman's fertility, marriage rituals and child rearing. By their intimate nature they remain something of an enigma despite much scholarly research. It is tempting to classify the dolls by their visual features but there are many crossovers between ethnic groups which blur the identification. The older dolls are rather abstract in their form, suggestive of their cultural group rather than representational in every detail.

Many are now made for the external market and have become miniature versions of their adult counterparts. The diversity of materials used by the makers included calabash, reeds, gourds, clay, discarded bottles, corn stalks and maize cobs combined with buttons, beads and fabric.

Gimwane (child figure)
Ntwane, South Africa
Fibre, beads, leather, plastic, tin, wooden core, wool, buttons.
Height: 29.7cm, diameter: 10.4cm.
Standard Bank African Art Collection.

Decoration

As inspiration for personal development it is the area of innovation and imaginative use of resources that is my focus here.

It is that ability to see possibilities in the unexpected and to devise innovative techniques that fuel the imagination. Paper clay is a versatile medium that I have recently discovered. It can be shaped or moulded rather like pastry and coloured before working or painted afterwards. I rolled some out flat to a thickness of about 2mm and cut out shapes similar to buttons, embossed them and pierced holes so that I could sew them onto fabric. They harden as they dry and are ready to be painted and then finished with lacquer or varnish if you want a ceramic effect. I experimented with acrylic inks, metallic paints and patina aging solutions to create these samples. You could try combining fabric and paper in the paper making process, with fabric being trapped between layers of paper pulp, as a way of creating a material.

In layering up surfaces there are opportunities to hide or trap items, partly concealing or revealing what is embedded underneath. Paper pulp can be moulded to create three dimensional forms and then stitched, stiffened or treated with mixed media. Finding a material that has the qualities that express your own ideas is sometimes a long and tortuous process. It's worth persevering and success can come from the most unexpected sources, if you are prepared to have a go! I experimented with combining paper pulp, fabric and metal and applying buttons made from paper clay. Here are some experiments at the beginning of that long journey.

Experiments with mixed media in progress.

Stephen Long

Fascination with beadwork started at the early age of five when a family friend showed Stephen some beaded artefacts. His interest grew, and inspired by visits to museums he started to buy some beadwork for his own collection and learn more about the Xhosa culture. On moving to the outskirts of Cape Town at the age of ten, Stephen met Thembesile Dyantyi, a Xhosa shepherd and herdsman, who encouraged his interest in his language and culture. In the past almost all Xhosa women who followed a traditional lifestyle, could bead in the distinctive style of their own district. They made beaded items for their own personal use or as gifts for their boyfriends or husbands. In 1983 Stephen made his first collecting trip to the Eastern Cape, formerly known as the Transkei. Beadwork was his main interest and the only aspect of material culture that was available at that time. The pieces he collected were examples made in the 1940s onwards and were often in need of repair. This was the motivation for learning about their construction so that he could repair and restore them and in the process he learnt much about their history and the enthralling story of beads. It encompasses the use of early beads from South India to Czech and Venetian beads and now to the cheaper Chinese glass beads and locally made plastic ones.

The traditional beading culture has been eroded by urbanisation, the influx of cheap mass produced goods and westernisation. Beadwork is now only made by *shamans* or diviners and some cultural groups who produce contemporary designs. Stephen is passionate about preserving good examples of historical pieces for posterity and also enthusiastic about teaching the techniques to the current generation before the skills are lost for ever. He says, 'The elderly women were my teachers and twenty five years later, I often end up teaching those techniques to their grandchildren in practical workshops.'

Stephen has chosen a choker or *ikhali* as his inspirational piece. It would have been worn by a young man of the Xhosa-speaking Mfengu group of people. The choker is worn around the neck, fastened by twisting the sinew around the mother-of-pearl buttons. The beaded leather streamers hang down on the chest and are decorated at the end with triangular pendants. It is a favourite piece in his collection because of its colours, the skilful and complex technique that creates a double layer of beads and the inclusion of the decorative streamers.

He collected it in the 1980s or early 1990s in a village on the outskirts of King William's Town in the Eastern Cape Province.

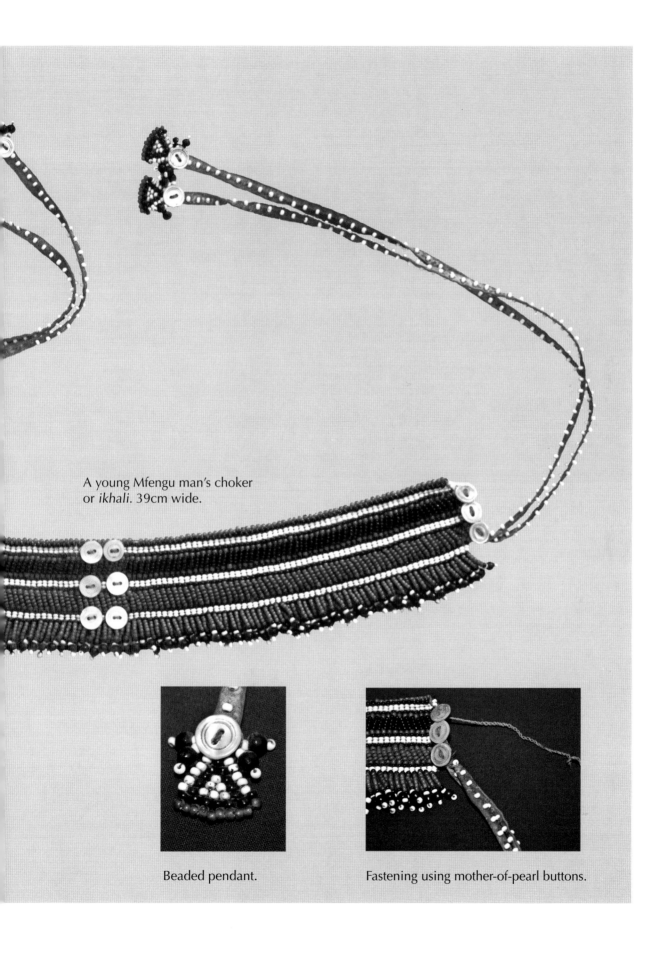

A young Mfengu man's choker or *ikhali*. 39cm wide.

Beaded pendant.

Fastening using mother-of-pearl buttons.

Chapter 5
Embroidery and Embellishment

Africa is an enormous continent and craft skills, designs, materials and methods of working vary widely across the regions. Embroidery is still practised in many parts of Africa. It is not confined to political borders, but related to groups of people, or traditional regional techniques. I am particularly interested in embroidery skills still practised in southern African countries and sub-Saharan regions. I have focussed on traditional craft skills in particular in regions where I have been able to experience their way of life at first hand. Museum textile and beadwork collections have also been a wonderful source of information. Studying them as sources of inspiration has made me realise that there is so much more yet to discover. In this chapter I have chosen a range of embroidered textiles and beadwork that show the love of colour, pattern and surface texture. This lively approach to design is expressed in everyday items as well as ceremonial pieces, such as the ceremonial raphia cloth you see here. Lines of surface stem stitch contrast with areas of Kasai velvet, a cut pile technique. These highly patterned and textured sections are balanced by plainer panels. Some are decorated with lines of knotted stitch and cowrie shells and another has more organic shapes worked in reverse appliqué.

A pieced raphia cloth from the Democratic Republic of the Congo 150 x 41cm.

For those who love stitched surfaces, Hausa embroidery is a feast! Some of their finest embroidered garments are magnificent robes. The Hausa live in northern Nigeria and the bordering country of southern Niger. For centuries trade routes have crossed their region, exposing them to many different cultures which have influenced their designs. The finest robes or *boubous* were made from hand spun cotton, local wild or imported silk or indigo-dyed cotton. A *boubou* is dramatic both in size and surface design and is worn by a man of some status. The Hausa often pass on these highly prized robes as family heirlooms.

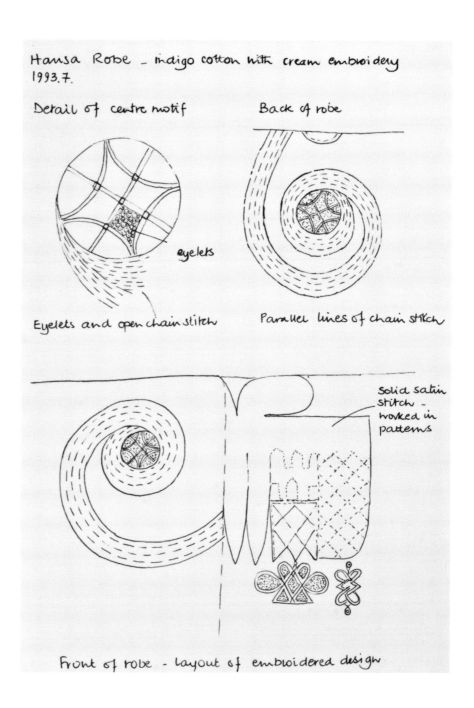

Hausa Robe - indigo cotton with cream embroidery
1993.7.

Detail of centre motif

Back of robe

eyelets

Eyelets and open chain stitch

Parallel lines of chain stitch

Solid satin stitch - worked in patterns

Front of robe - layout of embroidered design

Studies of a Hausa robe in the Embroiderers' Guild Collection.

Those worn by women are less flamboyant and tighter fitting, but also demonstrate highly developed skills. These voluminous robes for men can be as wide as four metres and are gathered at the shoulder when worn. They are rectangular in shape with openings in the side seams for armholes, and in the bottom seam for the legs. A *boubou*, or *riga*, its Hausa name, is worn over huge baggy trousers, drawn up at the waist and tightly fitting at the ankles. It is amazing to see the vast expanse of fabric created by joining lengths of strip woven cloth to form the shape of the robe. They are a stunning sight, seen at their best when billowing out and swirling rhythmically during a dance.

The surface embroidery is an inspiration and a joy to stitch enthusiasts. The elaborate, dense surface stitching is a distinctive feature of Hausa embroidery, and once seen, is instantly recognisable. Textile scholars suggest that the increasing use of embellishment and surface decoration is evidence of growing prosperity and increase their value as symbols of status and prestige. The elaborate embroidery is worked by men in asymmetric designs sweeping across the surface, to produce a sumptuous effect both on the back and the front. The decoration is concentrated on the areas around the neck opening, on the front chest sections and also the back.

Embroidery worked on strip-woven cloth – detail from a Hausa robe.

The neck opening showing the solid embroidery and indigo-dyed lining – detail from a Hausa robe.

The motifs include interlacing forms, bold angular shapes, circles, spirals and lines that cover large areas of the constructed strip woven surface. The combination of shapes and symbols include Islamic and oriental influences, as well as indigenous decoration found on Hausa pottery, basket work and body decoration. Some densely embroidered sections are worked separately and applied to strengthen the neck or pocket edge and are practical as well as decorative. The large shapes are worked in densely stitched rows of what looks like Romanian couching and others are filled with closely worked eyelets, known as 'a thousand ant holes.' These painstaking techniques are time consuming and so it is not surprising that the demand for these embroidered robes is now mostly met by using machine embroidery.

Hand embroidery on the front panel of a Hausa robe.

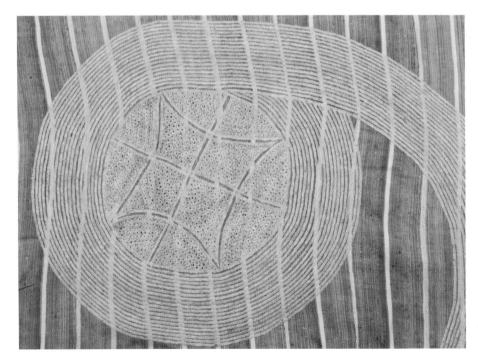

A circular symbol on a Hausa robe filled with eyelets.

There are several distinctive elements that come together to produce these intricately worked garments. It is these features that are of particular interest and suggest avenues to explore. The way that the sinuous, curving shapes sweep across the large expanse of fabric, created by the narrow strip woven lengths suggests ideas about background fabrics. Working across a pieced or striped ground fabric could lead to some interesting variations on a stitched surface. There are subtle changes of tone as embroidered areas cross a striped background, with an infinite number of combinations to explore. The rhythm of hand stitching lends itself to repeating a single type of stitch, in order to create lines or fill shapes.

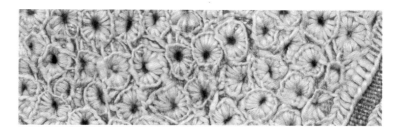

Detail of densely worked eyelets.

Inspired by the rich tactile surface in the Hausa robe shown here, I started to work on ideas using eyelets on their own. If you refer to a stitch dictionary you will see that there are several ways of doing this versatile stitch. Sometimes it is the hole rather than the surface stitch that is dominant. I chose to use the buttonhole stitch similar to those on the *boubou* to create the eyelets.

Here are some ideas to try:

» Use a variety of coloured threads, shiny and matt.

» Use space-dyed threads.

» Explore a range of threads from fine to thick.

» Overlap the stitches.

» Vary the size of the stitch.

» Try a formal arrangement or let it grow organically.

» Work on different weights of fabric.

» Use loosely woven fabrics.

» Use canvas or even weave fabric.

» Include a layer underneath to reveal a different colour through the eyelets.

» Experiment with the eyelet attachment on your sewing machine.

» Combine machine worked eyelets with hand stitching.

Embroidery and Embellishment

I discovered when I worked on canvas that the hole became more dominant and the regular grid resulted in a geometric effect with square, rectangular or diamond-shaped motifs. The design can be very formal and orderly, or more free, as you can see in the sample, where I used space-dyed threads on a fine canvas.

Perlé threads on even weave fabric.

Perlé threads on loosely woven cotton.

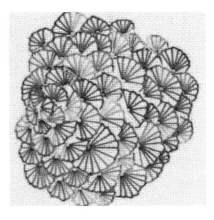

Space-dyed coton à broder on fine linen.

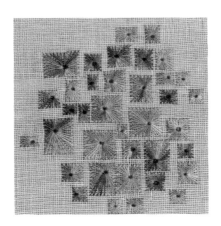

Space-dyed threads on fine canvas.

A variety of threads worked on sprayed canvas.

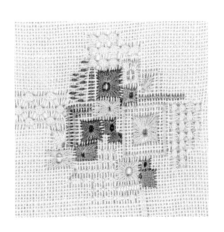

Stranded cotton on coarse linen.

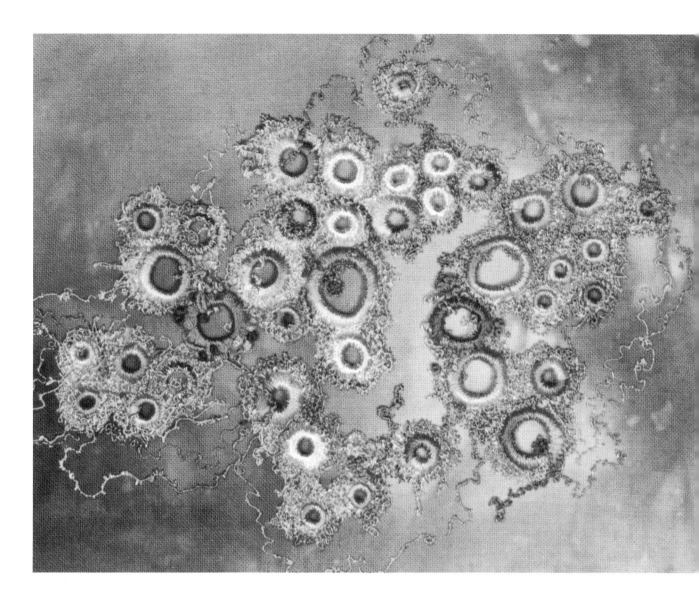

Machine stitched eyelets on space-dyed cotton.

Eyelets can be worked by hand, first piercing the fabric to create holes and then overcasting them to make the eyelet, a familiar technique used in white work. A similar effect can be achieved by using the eyelet attachment on the sewing machine. Using the attachment, I worked some eyelets directly on the ground fabric and others were worked separately, cut out and applied with free machine stitching and some hand embroidery.

The technique of packing stitches closely together, to form a richly embellished motif or textured surface is exploited very successfully in Nigerian hats as well as the robes. Some parts of the Hausa *boubous* are so densely stitched that they look as if they have been woven and perhaps it is no surprise to know that these embroidered robes are very valuable. They continue to be worn on special occasions such as weddings and funerals and also by people in high office as a mark of status and prestige.

A range of raphia cloths showing the use of eyelets.

Eyelets are a feature of raphia cloths too. The raphia cloths, known as Kasai velvets or Kuba cloths, are more often discussed for their cut pile technique and have been a source of fascination to scholars and artists for a long time. The complex patterns, rectilinear in form, made up from squares, chevrons, triangles and crosses are interesting, sometimes more for their irregularities than anything else! Ann Svenson, a museum textile conservator with an interest in Kuba textiles captures the qualities of these cloths:

> 'To western eyes, the cloths are simultaneously bold and intricate, dramatic and subdued, irregular and ordered, as well as asymmetrical and balanced. In all cases they are fluid, visually engaging and full of surprises.'

I recently acquired a long raphia cloth, which is a wonderful example of Ann Svenson's description. It has a contrasting colour palette in the cut pile sections, dramatic tonal variations, reverse appliqué using the knotted stitch and is embellished with knotted lines of embroidery and cowrie shells.

Part of a ceremonial raphia cloth from the Congo region showing the reverse appliqué and surface embellishment.

Embroidery and Embellishment

Patchwork is a familiar technique used in North America and Europe as a way of constructing a large textile from small geometric shapes. It is also used in the raphia cloth skirts from the Democratic Republic of the Congo. Finished cloths are worn at ceremonial occasions and their continued survival is mainly due to their importance at funeral celebrations. Piecing is combined with patchwork to create the raphia dance skirts, which may be as long as 12 metres. Sections of varying size are pieced together with patchwork. In the example shown here the patchwork is made up of natural and dyed rectangular pieces. Some patches have cutwork sections, others are embroidered with eyelets and surface stitches and some have been treated with stitch-resist dye techniques.

In more complex pieces the flat patchwork sections are joined to highly textured cut pile pieces and combined with various types of appliqué. They are finished by hemming, binding

Rectangular patchwork in a Kuba skirt using a variety of textile techniques.

or by adding a fringe. A tactile surface is achieved by all the finished edges being turned onto the right side. The surface is further enhanced by joining the sections with the knotted stitch described in Chapter 2, where I explain the method of joining small square patches to create a checkerboard effect.

The use of one fibre to weave the fabric, embroider and sew the patchwork together could be replicated in other ways. Creating a piece of patchwork by using one type of fabric for your patchwork and then combining patches treated with different techniques is well worth exploring. I have used woad-dyed fabric and threads to join the plain and tie-dyed rectangles in the sample shown here.

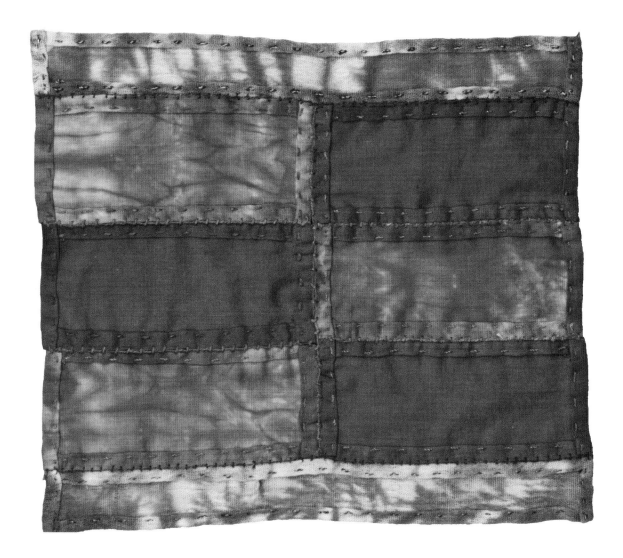

Patchwork using woad-dyed fabrics and thread.

Patching a hole.

Holes and worn areas in the surface of the raphia cloths were caused by pounding the cloths to soften them. Occasionally there was a practical need to repair a worn area and a patch was used to cover it. I have seen many examples where this is the case and a virtue has been made out of necessity.

The intricate stitched surfaces are seen at their best when the long cloths are wrapped around the body layer upon layer. Drawn and cutwork sections reveal underlying layers, lines of overstitching, and sprinklings of eyelets. The open work used in the raphia cloths is created by first removing warp or weft threads. Binding or wrapping the remaining threads creates an openwork lattice section in the ground fabric. Those of you who enjoy creating open work surfaces by machine can achieve similar effects by slitting or removing threads before using a zigzag to pull remaining threads together. This is very successful when worked freely by machine on a loosely woven fabric.

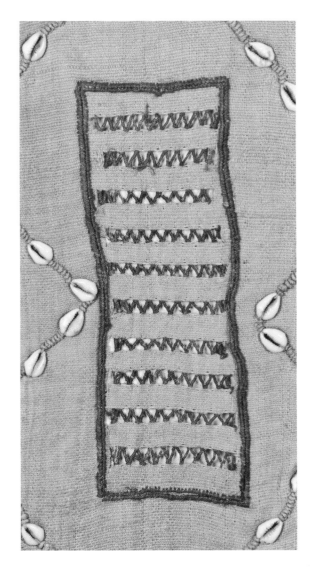

Openwork sections in a raphia cloth from the Congo region.

Bold effects can be achieved by using appliqué, especially when a contrasting colour is used. The technique offers the possibility of introducing curved or circular shapes as the woven grid of the ground fabric can be ignored. Many stylised forms appear in raphia cloths, but circular shapes are unusual in being found only on appliquéd cloths. Including them is particularly interesting, as the predominant structure of the designs is of interlocking geometric shapes.

Curved shapes used for appliqué on a ceremonial Kuba raphia skirt.

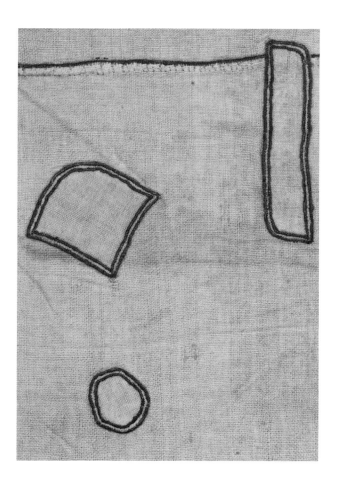

The knotted stitch, already mentioned gives a firm edge to appliquéd shapes and adds a decorative line as you can see in the examples shown here. It works equally well in reverse or inlay techniques. Where a bolder effect is required a solid double line of stitching is used instead. It is effective when the applied piece is of a similar tone to the ground fabric as in the *mapel* made by the Ngeende people of the Congo region. There is a subtle change of surface even though the same fabric has been used for the patch and the ground fabric. Instead of aiming for invisible stitching try these alternative ways of applying your motifs.

Shapes applied with a double line of stitching on a *mapel* from the Congo region.

Beadwork is widespread throughout Africa and many pieces are featured in this book, demonstrating the diverse ways in which beads alone are used to make a constructed fabric. Various types of netting, loom weaving and square stitch are techniques used for collars, beaded skirts, belts and covers for three-dimensional objects. Fringes, tassels and body ornaments are just some of the many examples of beaded decoration. Much of the beadwork worn by young Zulu men and women is concerned with courtship.

A Zulu *ucu*.

These small beaded decorations are intimate pieces and there is a widely held view that they contain messages which are private and personal to the people concerned. The small squares of beadwork hung on strands of beads or fastened with a pin are referred to as *ucu*, which translated, means love letter. The Xhosa also make love letter pins and pendants using simple patterns.

Favourite motifs are stars, trees, rivers or geometric shapes. They may be purely decorative, tell a story, represent a relationship, record the number of children in a family, or denote a personal quality, such as diligence. There are many now made for the tourist trade which have no profound meaning, but are attractive souvenirs.

An old Mfengu love letter
pendant.

 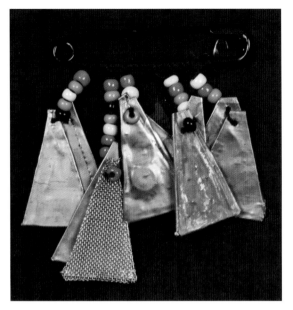

Safety pin brooches.

I have used safety pins to make similar items using some of my own hand made attachments using recycled copper and beads. However, there are also ways of embellishing fabrics by stitching beads on the surface rather like embroidery stitches. Lines and patterns can be applied with beads using the lazy stitch. Lazy stitch requires beads to be threaded to the length required and the thread taken through to the back of the fabric, coming through to the front at the beginning of the next stitch. They are often laid down in parallel rows to build up blocks of colour or worked in zigzag lines to form a pattern or a border. It is a simple and quick way of embellishing a surface, which is quite hard wearing, provided the 'beaded stitch' is not too long. The Thembu belt combines the lazy stitch with applied stripes of black fabric repeated to form a pattern on cotton baise.

Zigzag pattern on a Thembu beaded belt using lazy stitch.

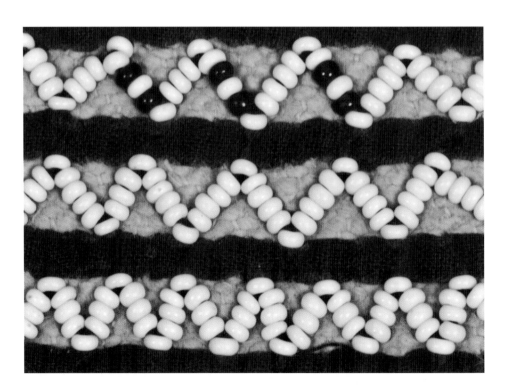

Appliqué stitch is similar, in that it can fill a shape or follow the contours of a design. You need two threads for this method of applying beads. One is threaded with beads and follows the lines of the design, while the other holds the first thread down at intervals with a small over stitch. Further embellishment is frequently added to the edges with a zipper edge, clover leaf end or divided strands. You can see examples of these in the bead sampler. I have also included shells and porcupine quills as surface embellishments.

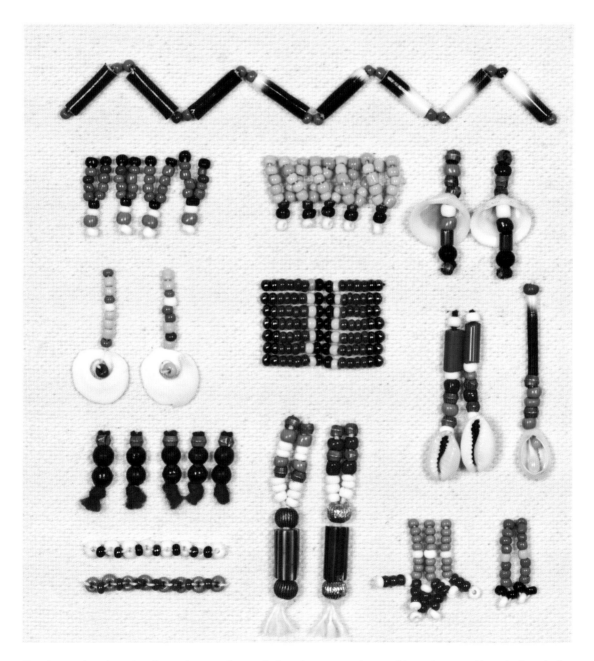

Bead sampler showing from the top: lazy stitch using porcupine quill sections and beads, beaded fringes, bead tassels with shells, a block of lazy stitch, bead fringes and zipper edges.

Embroidery and Embellishment

Fastenings are an opportunity for embellishment too! This young man's choker from the Msinga region of Kwazulu Natal makes a feature of the fastening with loops to fit over much larger red beads.

Fastening on a choker, Kwazulu Natal.

The Xhosa regularly use mother-of-pearl buttons with a cord to wind around the buttons as a method of fastening.

A cord would be wound round the buttons to fasten this Xhosa beaded girdle.

On beadwork necklaces and cascades there may be a beaded loop to fit over the button. Buttons are functional but are also regarded as decorative too. Frequently they are included as part of a surface pattern introducing a change of scale and surface to beadwork. This idea is used to great effect on the neck piece of the Xhosa neck cascade. Little white buttons cover the black cotton band and are attached with groups of six small beads to create an interesting texture and pattern. The bead cascade is made separately with loops to attach it to the neck piece.

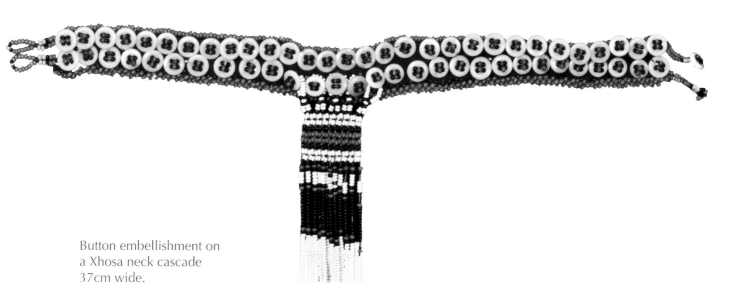

Button embellishment on a Xhosa neck cascade 37cm wide.

Embroidery and Embellishment

I love the idea of pattern making using buttons as a repeated shape and have tried several experiments using other ways of covering a surface with circular shapes. In the sampler shown I have used ostrich eggshell beads, shell discs, cowrie shells, sea shells and porcupine quills with traditional glass beads.

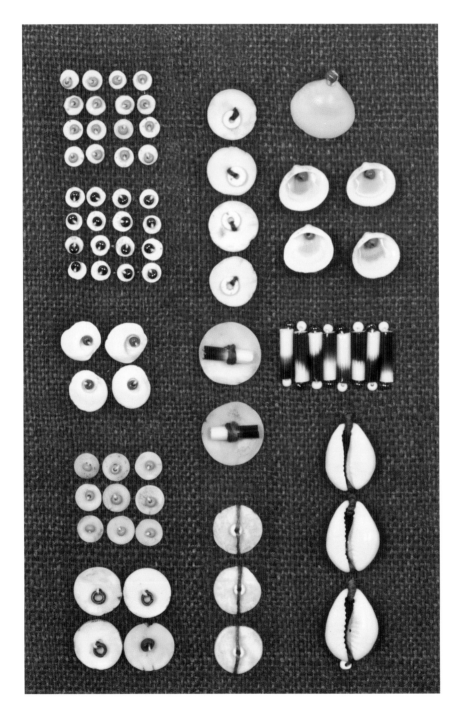

Experimental sampler using natural items attached with beads as embellishment.

Non-governmental organisations and craft cooperatives have been instrumental in providing training in skills, that women in particular, may use to generate income for their families. There are now many groups who are successfully producing hand crafted items for sale. Embroidery is a popular skill as hand stitching requires few resources or specialist equipment.

The image of the buck and the distinctive shape of the tree come from Rosinah's own environment with little importance given to scale. She has used brightly coloured perlé thread to fill the shapes with closely worked stem and satin stitch. Not only have women benefitted from the guidance and commitment of skilled practitioners but have also developed artistically, creating a style of their own as you can see in this naïve landscape. Success sometimes brings tensions and unexpected social consequences, so it is not just a simple matter of finding ways of putting the natural love of colour, pattern and texture into new and viable ways of working. There are social considerations. Some community based projects do succeed and become successful business enterprises.

A few years ago we came across one such project based in Cape Town. It employed less than twenty women, many of them immigrants from troubled areas in neighbouring countries. The women were also HIV/Aids positive so couldn't always work regularly. At that time they had been given a space in a building to work in the midst of the hurly burly of a factory floor.

Embroidered panel made by Rosinah Makhubela 33 x 17cm.

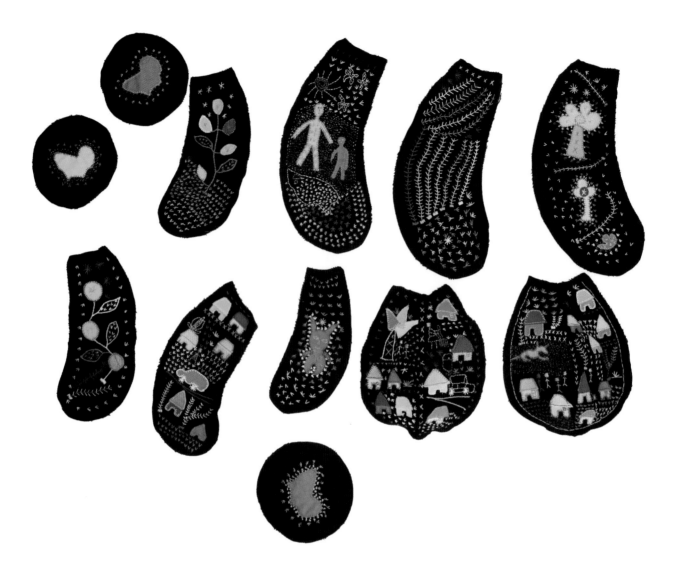

Details of embroidered pieces for a *Forward Bear*.

They formed a co-operative called *Forward Bears*, translated from the Xhosa for 'moving forward' and make wonderfully embroidered bears. They have learnt a wide variety of traditional embroidery stitches to decorate the individual pattern pieces that make up a bear.

These are sewn together to make up the body and stuffed to produce a highly decorated bear. It's a time consuming occupation using detailed hand embroidery to decorate the bears. These are bears with a difference! The ground fabric is black cotton and colourful threads are used to cover the body with a lively mixture of stitches and some beads. Since then the group have diversified and now include denim and *ishweshwe* fabric in their products. They are becoming well known and *Forward Bears* are now available through many retail outlets in Cape Town.

A Forward Bear.

Many traditional ways of working are being superseded by manufacturing processes and cheap imported goods are taking the place of hand made items. Market forces and easier communication influence people's choices in southern Africa just as they do across the world. However, it is encouraging that textile and embroidery techniques are being re-introduced as important elements in development projects. These provide employment in rural and urban communities and are based on local decorative traditions and skills. Craftsmanship, including embroidery, is alive and continues to evolve as it responds to the tourist trade, the wider concerns of market forces and the global economy.

Appendix
Instructions for making paper boxes

Making the boxes

The dimensions suggested here are suitable for using with the flour paste decorated papers on page 10 – 11 and the book cloth described on pages 87 - 88.

Cube Box

» Mark out the measurements on the wrong side of the paper or book cloth. The base measures 5cm square. Each side will be identical in size.

» Cut out the pattern and fold along the dotted lines.

» Cut along the four solid red lines towards the base as shown.

» Then fold in A, B, C, and D in the direction of the arrows to create the sides of the box.

» Fold E, F and G over the sides and glue the tabs to the base.

» Fold J in two to form a flap for the lid.

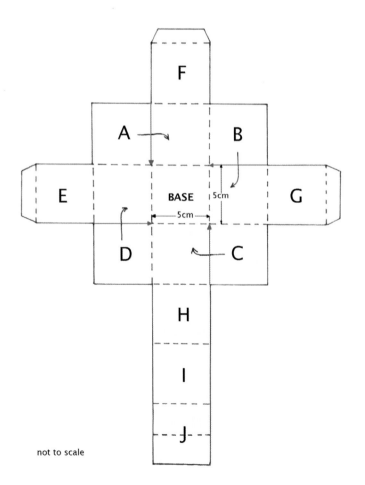

Cube box.

not to scale

» Fold I over H and glue together to form a double thickness for the top.
» Insert an eyelet in J to attach a tie if required.
» Cut a piece of card to fit into the base and glue it in position.

Shallow box with lid

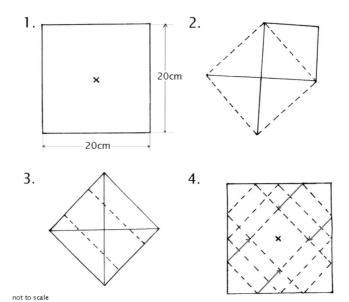

Shallow box with lid   not to scale

» Cut out a 20cm square of paper or book cloth for the box.
» Cut out a square 3mm larger for the lid.
» Mark the centre on the wrong side by drawing diagonals from opposite corners. (1)
» Fold all four corners to the centre mark and crease carefully. (2)
» Fold two opposite sides to the centre and crease. (3)
» Open the square out flat.
» Cut on the solid red lines to the square base from the sides. (4)
» Fold in any two opposite corners to the centre and bring up the sides to form two sides of the box.
» Tuck the corners round to form the other two sides and bring the other corners over them onto the base.
» They can be glued down and a piece of card cut to fit the base and give the box some strength.
» The lid is made in exactly the same way but is marginally bigger so that it fits over the box.

Bibliography

Bannister Anthony & Lewis-Williams David *Bushmen*
A Changing Way of Life Struik, Cape Town 1- 86825-178-0

Beckwith Carol & Fisher Angela *African Ceremonies 1 & 2*
Abrams Inc., New York 0-8109-4205-4

Blauer Ettagale *African Elegance* Struik, Cape Town
1-85368970-X

Carey Margret *Beads and Beadwork of East & South Africa*
Shire 0-85263-797-7

Elliot Aubrey *The Ndebele* Struik, Cape Town 1-86825-425-9

Elliot Aubrey *Tribal Dress* Struik, Cape Town 1-86825-424-0

Fisher Angela *Africa Adorned* Collins Harvill, London
00-0-216622-4

Gillow John & Sentence Bryan *World Textiles*
Thames & Hudson, London 0-500-01950-9

Haskins Jim & Biondi Joann *From Afar to Zulu* Walker & Co,
New York 0-8027-7550-0

Idiens Dale & Ponting K. G. (Eds) *Textiles of Africa*
Pasold Research Fund 0-903859-08-4

Jacobson Margaret *Himba Nomads of Namibia*
Struik, Cape Town 1-86872-130-2

Meurant Georges *Shoowa Design* Thames & Hudson, London
0-500-97331-8

Meyer Laure *Art & Craft in Africa* Terrail, Paris 03-45309-9

Morris Jean & Eleanor Preston-Whyte *Speaking with Beads*
Thames & Hudson, London 0-500-27757-5

Phillips Tom (Ed) *Africa, The Art of the Continent*
Royal Academy of Arts, London 3-7913-1603-6

Picton John & Mack John *African Textiles*
British Museum Publications, London 0-7141-1552-5

Turle Gillies *The Art of the Maasai* Alfred A Knopf,
New York 0-394-58323-X

Exhibition Catalogues:

Voice-Overs Standard Bank Art Collection University of the
Witwatersrand Art Galleries, South Africa 1-86838-344-X

Evocations of the Child Johannesburg Art Gallery,
Human & Rousseau, South Africa 0-7981-3830-0

Democracy X University of South Africa Unisa Press,
South Africa 1-86888-325-6

Contributors & Suppliers

Contributors:

Stephen Long
stephen_longst@yahoo.com

Binky Newman
binky@mweb.co.za

Mary Sleigh
www.lizard-dance.com

Dyes and patinating solutions:

Art Van Go
01438 814946
www.artvango.co.uk

Kemtex Colours
01257 230220
www.kemtex.co.uk

Teresinha Roberts
07979 770865
www.woad.org.uk

Fabrics and threads:

MacCulloch & Wallis
020 7629 0311
www.macculloch.com

Oliver Twists
0191 416 6016

The African Fabric Shop
www.africanfabric.co.uk

The Silk Route
01252 835781
www.thesilkroute.co.uk

Whaleys (Bradford) Ltd
01274 576 718
www.whaleys-bradford.ltd.uk

Book binding papers, eyelets, tools and sundries:

Shepherds Bookbinders & Falkiners
Fine Art Papers
www.falkiners.com

Bags of Handles
01394 279868
www.bagsofhandles.co.uk

Index

MARY SLEIGH
EMBROIDERER